# MOTHER WARNED YOU
## Tantrum, Cottonmouth, Mike's Place

*Erick W. Miller*

authorHOUSE®

*AuthorHouse™*
*1663 Liberty Drive*
*Bloomington, IN 47403*
*www.authorhouse.com*
*Phone: 1-800-839-8640*

*First published by AuthorHouse 4/27/2011*

*ISBN: 978-1-4567-6050-2 (e)*
*ISBN: 978-1-4567-6048-9 (hc)*
*ISBN: 978-1-4567-6049-6 (sc)*

*Library of Congress Control Number: 2011906619*

*Printed in the United States of America*

# Thoughts and quotes from the author;

"Everything you do, do as a Christian. If anything goes wrong, it won't be your fault." To all my children from 2009 forward.

"The worst thing you can think of has already happened. It can happen again, *and*, it can happen to you!" Circa 1985

"Life is easy if you don't follow the rules. Dying is easier if you do." 10 August 03

"'Courage' is doing what should be done, even if you're afraid. 'Integrity' is doing what needs to be done even if you stand to gain nothing, regardless of the cost to you." 10 August 03

"There are no such things as werewolves and vampires. There are lions, tigers, bears, and gorillas. However, the scariest thing on the face of the earth is man. Some day, son, you will be the scariest thing on the planet." Spoken to my oldest son Travis W. Miller after his fourth birthday. Circa 1978

"If you think something is wrong, *it is*. Don't do it!" Circa 1982, again, me, to all my children, oft' repeated.

"If you're going to do something stupid, do it alone because a partner is a witness!" Advice given to one of my struggling Christian acquaintances. Circa 1980

"Of course I know the value of a dollar. A dollar is worthless. If you don't have your health, if your children don't love you, if you have no friends, what good is a dollar!" Excerpt of conversation from 1978

"The devil doesn't care if you believe in him or not, as long as you do his work. You can either put bricks in the house of the Lord, or in the house of the devil." Spoken and oft' repeated to all of my children. Circa 1978 to present...

"The stakes have always been the same since the Garden of Eden. You have your life, your health, your family, and your immortal soul." Reply to statement, "The stakes are so much higher today." circa 1985

"There's no such thing as a <u>coincidence</u>." Author unknown.

The stories in this book, all of its characters and contents are purely fiction, created by Erick W. Miller. Any resemblance to anyone living or dead is unintentional and merely a <u>coincidence</u>. They say that a little bit of the author goes into each of his characters. I think that is a gross understatement.

"THERE IS NO SUCH THING AS A COINCIDENCE!"
THE SCARIEST THING ON THE FACE OF THE EARTH
IS MAN!

# CONTENTS

# TANTRUM

Now that my Blazer was sold and my 1990 Chevy Pickup was loaded with all my worldly goods, I was ready for the ritual. First I would say a prayer that my beater would start. Then I would turn the key. I was joking! I take care of my vehicles. Here I was at fifty-six starting over, again, yes, again. I was getting good at starting over. Someday I would like to know how it felt to finish something. My first stop was a gas station. This big truck wasn't very economical but it ran well and there were no payments. It was Halloween. Now was a good time to head south before winter really got started in Racine, Wisconsin where I'd been living for two years. I was aiming for the Phoenix metropolitan area. I'd grown very fond of that place after my first of many visits. I missed the desert, and now I was doing something about it.

People who say that getting there is half the fun aren't as tired of the long drive as I am. I like to start my journey just before sundown. I go straight south rather than cut diagonally and therefore a shorter route. From the Memphis area, I use the interstate routes 40, 30, 20, and 10 into Phoenix metro. I'd even dropped south on I-45 out of Dallas a time or two in order to pick up I-10 in Houston, another place I was very fond of. Either way, it allows me to cross the continental divide at a mere four thousand feet instead of the dizzying heights along the northern route I-40 through Flag and south on I-17, or the shortcut from Holbrook through Payson and down State Route 87, the Beeline Highway. Switchbacks are hard on brakes and transmissions. The climate gets warm faster when I use this southern route. I positively love warm weather and I missed it, plain and simple.

New Mexico is a highly under rated state that the residents lovingly call the "Land of Enchantment". As a teenager, I had the opportunity to hitch hike from El Paso to Albuquerque and back. I was amazed at the temperature differential between night and day. Bitter, bone chilling cold at night and cozy warm sunny days. That was in October. I remember standing on top of a puddle of ice frozen solid to the ground wearing a T-shirt comfortably at 9:30 AM during that minor and eye opening adventure.

The route that I was driving on this trip wouldn't take me anywhere near Albuquerque. I would only pass through the narrow southern portion of the state between Texas and Arizona. The toughest part of the trip in my heavily laden truck would be Texas Canyon in southeastern Arizona. That part of the trip was a good reason not to make the drive in summer. I've put my vehicles through all kinds of torture traveling the desert states at the wrong time of year.

I had worked all day to finish a roofing job. I went to the bank, to a restaurant, then showered and started my trip. For lack of sleep, I spent the night in the Memphis area at a cheap motel on the Arkansas side of the river. Roofing will wear a man out, especially if you top it off with an eleven hour long trip on the interstate. Actually, I had no problems staying awake. I did have serious problems getting to sleep and remaining asleep. Stopping was just something that I felt like doing. So I did.

Feeling better after I woke up, I did some pushups and sit ups, then took another shower. I was starving. I dressed in my usual army pants and boots and black tank top. I'd long since given up on trying to impress anyone. The 101st Airborne Screaming Eagle and Combat Infantry Badge decals on my truck's back window completed the picture. I was a veteran and proud of that fact.

November first in that part of the country was still pretty warm, especially this year. The tank top might look out of place to the locals, but the air seemed downright balmy after Racine.

So, with some sleep, a shower, and a smile, I signed out of my overnight refuge and walked next door to the inevitable restaurant. I had slept so late that the breakfast crowd was already gone. No problem, I don't get along well with strangers. An empty restaurant was for the better.

The only waitress was on the phone. I could tell from her laughter and conversation, which she made no effort to conceal, that it was a personal call of little consequence. After a few minutes of being ignored, I went to the front counter and got a menu, then took my seat again. There are a limited number of ways to prepare a western omelet, which was all I wanted anyway, but I stared dutifully at the menu just in case I'd missed something. I made a big deal of closing the menu. She watched the entire charade without batting an eye. Too bad her Momma didn't do that very thing more often when she was a kid. Bat her in the eye.

I tried to look nonchalant, but truth be known, I was mad enough to kill. That's how I get, mad enough to kill, and it doesn't take long. Sometimes, just a heartbeat or blink of an eye is long enough time for me to go from calm to adrenaline-superman. Anyway, I walked out of the door casually, got in my truck, and went in search of another greasy spoon.

I said that I was starving when I awoke. Then, it was an exaggeration. Now, an hour later and sixty plus miles west on I-40, I was, starving that is. Aha, there was a freeway sign depicting the knife and fork logo telling travelers, even if they couldn't read English, that food was available at this exit. Liberals had succeeded in making our highways user friendly for terrorists, illiterates, and illegal aliens alike. To hell with political correctness!

I would eat just about anything at this point, but I was hoping for a 'sit down' restaurant where someone would kiss my butt like they gave a darn. Anyway there was the usual array of junk food palaces vying for their piece of the fast food pie. I was in luck. I spotted a family restaurant in front of a strip mall. It was just close enough to lunchtime that the parking lot was full. Great! More people for me to rub elbows with, just what I needed.

I should have opted for a drive through lane at one of the competitors, but I have this penchant for getting my butt kissed like I'm somebody with money to spend so their jobs have meaning and their boss turns a profit so he can pay everybody on Friday. I didn't expect anybody to kiss my butt literally, just sort of figuratively. I thought that they might at least hang up the phone long enough to see if I was a customer or just someone who inspects tables at strange restaurants. Being alone, like I usually was, due to my charming personality... There was that, and the difficulty I seemed to have finding a woman that I could trust. Anyway it was easy for them to find me a seat in the no smoking section which is the only place where I dine, or not at all, period. There I sat in my black tank top with my square shoulders and suntan.

The joint was as crowded as the parking lot evidenced. The booth across from mine was filled with construction workers. They smelled like beer, they were loud, and they were smoking. Now, I was still mad from that first waitress ignoring me and I was very, very hungry. I'm like a baby when it needs food. We both get crabby. It was probably a dumb move, but I pointed out that they were sitting in the non-smoking section. There were only four of them, but I could have sworn that I heard "Screw you" or words to that effect at least ten times. It was probably acoustics or something.

Anyway, their message was clear. That was a very difficult moment for me. Holding my temper is always an effort. I'd learned the hard way long ago that security cameras are everywhere. I stood up and said quietly that I'd be waiting outside for any and all that thought they were tough. It turned out that they all thought they were tough, all four of them.

There I was, outside, in back, where they followed me, all of them, with no, I repeat, zero security cameras. It occurred to me that anything that I did to keep from getting hurt would be A-OK. They wasted time bragging about what they were going to do to me. Me, I'm alone, shorter than the smallest one, with no, that's another zero, time to waste. I spotted weapons everywhere. I only hoped for enough time to use them **ALL** on each and every one of those loud-mouthed tough guys. Their big talk gave me much longer than the usual heartbeat or eye-blink that I required to turn into an animal.

I hoped that I didn't kill any of them simply because I didn't want to go to prison, not because I gave a damn about any of their worthless lives. At any rate, I was the last one standing, and the whole shooting match only took about two minutes. It seemed longer, but time has a way of standing still when I lose my temper. It seems like I'm the only one in regular time and everyone else is moving in slow motion.

What have I done? They were all so still as they lay there.

Once again, I was leaving a restaurant hungry, so much for blending into society. This time I cruised a drive through and hardened my arteries a little more, eager to get out of Dodge before the police, who were now at the restaurant, spotted me.

I made it through that adventure without a scratch, but the next time I stopped for gas, my whole body was sore like I had fallen from someplace high. I must have put some moves on those jerks. Strange, but I didn't remember much about it except for how quiet they were when I left. That, and how hungry I was.

I really couldn't remember too much about the details. It was always like that. It was not an out of body experience. It was an out of mind experience. Oh, that's rich! I made myself laugh out loud at the thought. Now I was in a good mood, but I was still alone. That's why I quit carpentry and started roofing for myself, so I could work alone. I was tired of holding myself back when I really wanted to kill anyone and everyone who got in my face.

Driving long distances alone provides one much time for thought. That last tantrum at the restaurant scared me. I really didn't know if any of them were dead. None of them were moving when I stopped. I don't stop if anyone is moving, unless someone is obviously trying to surrender, which *has* happened. When I sense fear, I back off. I'm not a bully. This time, I couldn't honestly remember if any of them tried to quit or run. I just kept throwing stuff and clubbing people until it got quiet except for my breathing. I remember how loud my breathing was. There had been blood, pretty much too. A little even got on me, yet I had no injuries.

I think it was time for me to see a shrink at the nearest VA hospital. Maybe when I got to Phoenix. Yeah, someday I would do that very thing. I know that I should and I will, later. Until then, there would be no more restaurants or crowded places for me.

I had stayed put in Racine two years in a row deliberately to build up a bank account. When a man has only himself to feed, that is usually an easy thing to do, as long as work is available in his field. I'd raised two children and two stepchildren. The youngest was twenty and on her feet. She had finally moved out of my *second* ex-wife's home. The second ex was another story. She cheated. Her sisters convinced her, a little too easily, I might add, that I had been cheating too. I wasn't.

I stayed single, or at least not committed, for three years. Then I met ex number three. Duh! I fell for the promise of undying love, again. So, I found myself raising another son, hers by some real jerk, her ex- husband. That wife beater is lucky he never met me. My new son turned out to be a fine young man. It saddens me a lot to admit it, especially to myself, but I actually spent more time raising my two stepchildren than I got to spend with my two natural children. I gave as much of myself to them as I could. Still, it was rougher for them. Of course I still love them and see them when I can. Better than that, they love me back. That goes for all four of them. My children's love is my reason for living. Well, that and women!

My stepson was in the army protecting his old man along with the rest of America. My oldest son was an electrician in Mesa, Arizona living with his wife and kids. My stepdaughter was living in Payson, Arizona with my oldest daughter and her children. Now my secret is out. My name is Evan Mullen and I'm a grandfather. You know, like, "My name is Joe Blow and I'm a dope freak." It was a joke. So it wasn't funny. Hey, I paid my dues. *I was a dope freak*, but I straightened up and I did it without a single meeting. Well, I had a meeting with the Lord. In my mind you know. There were no burning bushes, just a promise that I made. He fulfilled his side of the bargain when he saw that I was keeping my promise, but not until He was sure of me. I was sorely tested after that. Oh, and my name isn't Evan Mullen, I made that up. Until I find out the health status of the four smokers from the restaurant, I have to remain anonymous. Oh, you thought I made all of this up? Silly you. Read on.

Ah, heartburn. I was so used to eating healthy foods that the fare at the junk food palace gave me indigestion. My next meal would be at a Subway. Right now I felt more like barfing than eating.

"D" as in "daylight" is for driving which is what I was doing and would be for some time to come.

. . .

It had been dark for quite a while. My indigestion had finally given way to hunger again. Visions of a foot-long ham and turkey with all the vegetables were dancing in my head like the sugarplums were supposed to (but never did) when I was a kid and Disney was king of my brain. Elvis was king of my Mom's brain. He was cool, but I was into Disney, and girls, not just any girls, I was into **ALL** of them. I have preferences, but all it takes is a smile really. Now you know my weakness.

Annette Funicello on the Mickey Mouse Club made me glad to be a man, or a boy anyway. Ah, the fantasies! The poor dear never got to meet me. As a child, I wanted to marry my mother. Then I saw Marilyn Monroe and Jayne Mansfield and Jane Russell. I wanted all of them. Yep, all of them, at once. Hey, a man has to die from something.

Eerrrrrrrrt! That's the sound my tires made as I swerved onto a ramp in the midst of my dreams of (better not go there). I had seen a Subway logo lit up at a truck stop. Oh no, more people! Maybe I could put on a hat and just keep my eyes down, dodging foot traffic and avoiding trouble. Nah, that doesn't sound like the man I love, (Oops, I almost gave you my name, lets stick to Evan Mullen) Yeah, it didn't sound like the man I love, Evan what's his face. Salivating like Pavlov's dogs, I found a parking place near the door. (I'm going to use sauntering here.) I was sauntering in nonchalantly, trying not to look like I thought I was bad because sometimes guys ask you if you think you're bad. Anyway, there I was, wimpy old Evan what's-his-face sauntering in the door when I spied the girl of my dreams. She looked like all three of the aforementioned honeys except for she was more my age, maybe a little older. She had aged well and managed to look healthier and sexier than half of today's college girls. This lady cared about her looks. This enhanced her natural beauty. She worked here and she was smiling at me. You know, me Evan, heh heh.

My first fantasy made me shiver violently. She noticed and her smile started to fade. She looked worried now, so I smiled and said (comma quotation marks) I had a chill. (quotation marks) Actually, as you already know, I didn't, have a chill, but she bought it, looking relieved and smiling anew. I had a really dumb thought, something like "Here's ex to be number four" and actually laughed out loud. Her worried look came back. "I'm hungry and I love you," I blurted out, unable, or at least unwilling, to stop myself. She laughed now too.

You're not gonna believe this, but her name tag read, "Marilyn". Thought I was gonna die laughin'. I had to share the joke with her before the worried look came back. She took it as a compliment. That's what it really was anyway. Yeah, those ladies were hot and so was this one. I volunteered my name, the real one, and reached across the counter to shake her hand. She had on a pair of disposable gloves but shook my hand anyway. Her turn to laugh out loud. Beautiful, sexy, no wedding band, and a sense of humor, this was the real thing. Forget the popular soft drink claiming that title. She was the **REAL** thing. I was in love.

"Marilyn, dahling, what time does your beautiful self get off?" I asked, leaving her a comic opening that I hoped she picked up on.

Laughing again, she said, "That depends on you, big boy!" She laughed some more, looking into the windows to my soul as she said it.

The cards were on the table and (another cliché follows) the ball was in my court. "Sugar, you can get off as soon and as often and as hard as you want with me." She stopped laughing, but her smile 'spoke volumes'. (Damn cliché's!)

Still smiling, but serious now, she said, "My ride arrives at midnight, but I'll call him and cancel, for you." I almost shivered again, when she said that, looking straight into my eyes.

"Sugar, midnight can't come soon enough. I'd wait a week just to hold your hand." I was laying it on thick. She knew it. She loved it. She was mine. I was hers. It was only a matter of hours. Finally I ordered my sandwich sans onions so as not to spoil the evening. I could feel my arteries getting soft, so I got a bag of barbecue chips to cover that base.

Light years later, at midnight, I helped her clean up. Her ride, Darryl, decided to show up anyway. He was a big dude, maybe five years older than I was, with the soft gut of a man who depended on his bulk to intimidate people. My rock hard construction worker's body and thousand-yard stare were enough to convince him that his bluff wouldn't work. He took his gut, cowboy hat, and cigarette out the door after saying goodnight to Marilyn and casting a pitiful attempt at a glare in my direction.

The big dude had driven off in a 'Cowboy Cadillac' that looked new. Besides duel tires, it had more bells and whistles than the Pentagon's latest toy. That barstool cowboy was rolling in dough, yet Marilyn was climbing into my old pickup like it was a limousine. I would remember that fact. I promised myself not to let this woman down.

Marilyn let on that Darryl was her ex-husband. She said that he claimed to still be in love but that she knew better. She said that he had taught her a lesson and she wasn't forgetting it. I thought about asking her what the lesson had been, but I figured that she'd tell me by and by. Home for her was an older model single-wide mobile home in a trailer park. It looked to me like she had let Darryl keep his money when she left him. I'd be willing to bet that she was only renting.

The place was real clean inside. There were no pictures of kids in sight, but there was a photo of her with a black eye that she took down right away, but not soon enough.

"I saw that shiner in the picture. If you want to tell me about it, I'm a good listener," I said sincerely. I meant it too. I already figured out that Darryl was the tough guy who punched her and I figured that it was because she had called him on cheating. I also figured that she kept the picture around to remind her not to let him in anymore.

I also figured that she wasn't used to having strangers over or that picture would have been in another room. I could be wrong, but that's what I figured.

She asked me if I wanted a drink, which I didn't, and said so. She commented that Darryl drank too much. I was invited to watch her TV while she showered. I would have rather showered with her than watch TV, but... I wasn't invited and I've learned that patience and respect will get a man far.

When I clicked the remote, the Fox News Channel came on, another plus. I would have searched for that very station anyway. So, she and I thought a lot alike and we got along well from the start. Now I was glad that I wasn't much of a drinker. Only now did it occur to me that she might have been testing me with her offer of having one.

In a little while, she called to me from her bedroom. She was blow drying her hair in an attractive and sexy robe. She asked if I wanted to shower next. Great! I went out to the truck for a change of clothes. When I came out of the shower, she was fixed up real nice. I got the signal that she wanted to go out steppin'. I wasn't wearing my usual outfit. After I showered, I put on some blue jeans and a short sleeved black shirt with a two-button top, which I left open. The black Jungle Boots were back on though. They were the only shoes I owned except for some sneakers and a junky pair of hiking boots. Reading her mind, or so I thought, I asked her if she liked to dance. Her eyes lit up. It made me feel good to make her happy. It had slipped my notice, but it was Friday night. I was so used to working six or seven days per week taking holidays only when I ran out of work, that Friday and Saturday usually passed by unnoticed.

My heart was in my mouth at the thought of socializing with strangers, but I'd try to hold my temper and do it for this very special lady. I wanted to make her smile a lot. She directed me to a nightclub that had a full time country band. Some of the folks did line dancing. Most just danced free style, which I preferred.

Marilyn was a terrific dancer any style. She had a few drinks. I think, or at least I hope that she was gearing up her courage to spend the night with a stranger. On the way back from the bar, at closing time, she managed to squeeze her beautiful self in the center seat belt. It made me feel good that a woman would want to sit next to me again. It made me feel especially good, all over as a matter of fact, that this particular woman wanted to sit next to little old me. Yeah, I was feeling good *all* over, better than good in some spots.

So there we were, sitting real close, feeling real good, and getting real near to her trailer park. The conversation was at a trickle now. She was kind of quiet, but it was a good kind of quiet. I think both of us were anticipating happily our arrival at her home, our arrival and what was to follow. This was the happy picture. She and I, headed to the Casbah together.

"Son of a bitch!"

Don't look at me. She said it. I saw why at the same time that I heard it. Darryl's fancy pickup truck was parked in front of her home along with another less fancy one.

Now it was my turn, "**Son of a bitch**!" I meant it too. I could feel the anger rising like some uncontrollable beast. I knew something bad was about to happen, something very bad.

Remember earlier when I said how crabby I got when I was hungry? That's nothing. Mess with my woman or my sex life and then I get positively scary. Immediately I get scary. Marilyn was unbuckled and out of the truck before I was parked properly. She looked a little scary too. I heard her say that the other truck was Slim's.

The door to her trailer opened and Darryl's bulk filled the opening temporarily. Behind him came Slim, who wasn't. No sir, the dude behind Darryl, all the way, if you get my drift, was not slim at all and he was a head taller than the rich man in the cowboy hat who was trespassing at my new sweetheart's home. I said before that Darryl was big. Slim was two sizes up from that. If I had to guess, I'd say that he was six-foot-six barefoot, which he wasn't. The work boots he wore must have required the hides from half a herd of cattle. He was a lot younger than Darryl too.

Slim was yelling, "Where is the little punk?" Marilyn was yelling, "You son of a bitch!" Darryl was yelling, "You whore!" I felt left out since I wasn't yelling. I was, however, *thinking*. You've heard the saying, "My mind was racing." Mine was. I'm actually an intellectual. Not many people know that. Marilyn's dilemma had obviously become my problem too.

I figured that I would have five or six minutes at the most before the cops arrived. I'm sure that one or several of the neighbors had called as soon as the yelling started. I thought I could handle everything in front of me in about four and one half minutes, including the part where Marilyn grabs her prized possessions and we hightail it the hell out of here.

I kept the upright member of a bumper jack behind the seat. My baby brother taught me that trick. That's what I stabbed Slim in his humongous gut with. It is also what I hit him over the head with. Real hard too. Remember, I was trying to get done in *my* time schedule. If the gorilla got up, it would slow everything down. Darryl stopped yelling when he saw Slim out for the count, or maybe longer. He started running away in his pointy toed, big heeled, slippery soled cowboy boots. They looked like Noconas. Anyway, the jerk fell. He started begging for his life. I told Marilyn to grab what was near and dear to her and throw it in the truck.

"I can't be here when the cops come", I told her quietly but convincingly. She grasped the big picture and flew inside. Before she was up the stairs, I leaned down in Darryl's weak face and told him that if I ever saw him again, his funeral would be a closed casket affair.

"If you tell the cops anything about me, or who did this, I'll torture you before I set you on fire. Then I dropped a hammer blow on his nose, guaranteeing not one, but two black eyes. "That's for punching Marilyn," I hissed in his face, which he had now covered with his hands. I'm not sure if he heard me, but I felt better having said it. The main thing is that he heard and believed the part about his horrible death if he ratted me out.

The cops came roaring into the trailer park as we were pulling quietly and unobtrusively out. That was too close. No notice was taken of us, thank God. Oh yeah, I thank the Lord for a lot of things. Believe it or not, I am a devout Christian. I really am a very nice man. I just have a bad temper. Don't mess with me and everything will be everything, and nothing more.

So, with the upright part of my jack back behind the seat, we commenced to un-ass the area with all of my stuff and Marilyn's most prized possessions. She evidently didn't have too much that she cared about.

She was laughing excitedly as we got back on the interstate. "Little Rock is just down the road. Can we get a room there?" Marilyn asked as if reading my mind.

"I was hoping you'd ask, Sugar," I replied. "First, I have to do something important. Slim's DNA is on that metal bar I hit him with.

That has to disappear." I used the very next exit that wasn't all lit up. It was just a highway in the middle of nowhere. I followed it to a long straight stretch of desolate nowhere, stopping only when I could see no headlights in either direction. My tools were easy to reach near the tailgate. I grabbed a two-pound mall and pounded the jack handle quickly into the soft ground of the ditch.

Before long, I was checking us into a tiny place with the ominous sounding name of "Silent Night Motel." We got to know each other inside out right up until five-thirty the next morning. We had an awful lot in common. Our appetites for each other were equally matched. I let her shower first while I did my sit ups and push-ups. She came out and caught me. She told me she was happy to see that I took my health and fitness so seriously.

I signed us up for another night before we went to breakfast. We had to drive a ways south on the county highway to get to the little town where the diner was. It was a poor farming community. These were my people, honest and hard working. I didn't expect, nor did I find any trouble there. All the men looked at my beautiful friend, something I *did* expect, but no one got rude.

Marilyn and I ate like there was no tomorrow. When we returned to the Silent Night Motel, sleep was our number one priority.

I woke up to rain. It was late afternoon and Marilyn was still sleeping. She was as beautiful sleeping as she was awake. I slipped out of bed quietly and headed for the bathroom. When I came out, Marilyn was at the window, peeking out of the drapes. She smiled happily when she turned toward me.

"You weren't in bed when I woke up and I was afraid that you'd left me," she confessed. "I'm sorry for thinking that you'd abandon me. I'm really lost and confused right now. I guess you could say that I'm homeless. I'm really quite frightened."

"Dear," I felt that I could call her that after what transpired over the last twenty-four hours, "As long as you want to stay with me, you'll have a roof over your head. True, we are currently homeless, but I'm not broke, plus I'm a journeyman carpenter and roofer. If you want to come to Arizona with me, we'll be just fine." That speech put her at ease. I could see the tension draining out of her. I finished my speech with, "Let's take a shower. We can wash each other's backs." That put the smile back on her face.

An hour or so later, as we cuddled up to each other. She asked me why I couldn't be there when the police arrived. I didn't want to lie, so I just said, "When I know you better, I'll tell you more about me. Right now, all you need to know is that I'll never be mean to you or abandon you and we'll never go hungry or sleep in the rain."

She was quiet for a bit which worried me. "Okay," was all she said. I felt her relax. I hadn't noticed it, but she must have been tense. She was trusting her fate to me and I wouldn't let her down. I'd been through so much in my life that it was easy for me to put myself in someone else's shoes. As far as understanding women, I'm pretty obviously the wrong person to give a lecture on how their minds worked. See? I can be honest with myself.

We showered again and managed to get our clothes on without assaulting one another. I figured that she was as hungry as I was, so I asked her what she liked to eat. After a short bout of laughter, which I caught from her, she said that she'd be happy with just about anything. She still managed to cling to a small part of being a little girl, which I admired her for. That's when I took off my money belt and dug out five folded one hundred dollar bills and gave it to her.

"Here Sugar, if anything happens to me, at least you're not broke or stranded," I said. "I will warn you that the police are going to want to know what made you abandon your home and lifestyle if you were thinking about going back in a pinch."

"My parents are long dead. I have no children, no brothers, and no sisters. That jerk Darryl was the only thing like family that I had left. He had me over a barrel and took advantage of my predicament. The people at Subway will wonder, as will the people who owned the restaurant where I worked during the day. Oh yes, I worked two jobs. I don't have a lazy bone in my body. I, too, managed to save a little money. Evidently it isn't as much as you, but I'm not broke either. I'll give you back this money when we get to Arizona. Thank you for making me feel safe and secure and thank you trusting me and just thank you for being here, now," said the new light of my life.

She seemed to be on the verge of tears, so I hugged her hard and long. Everything about her was so right for me. I hope she didn't change on me like all the others had. At any rate, we had thrown our lives together and I really liked it. Where had this woman been all my life? (I had so hoped I was done with clichés!)

We checked out of the eerily named Silent Night motel and drove to the diner in the little farming town again. We had both agreed that these people could use the business. Besides, the food was good and we were hungry. The drive seemed longer than I remembered from our last visit. When the highways were turned into freeways and re-routed, a lot of towns simply dried up and blew away. I prayed that it would never happen here.

We arrived to a sparse supper crowd. Even then, most of the customers were just sipping coffee to socialize with their neighbors. The poverty was evident. Their clothes were worn and long out of date but everyone was clean. Folks here took care of themselves and had accepted their lots in life cheerfully. I'd be surprised if one dime of the local money came from welfare.

The people were so likable as to make Marilyn and me feel at home, but my family was in Arizona and I missed them. Besides, people around here were hungry enough without having to assimilate two more adults into their fragile economy, sucking up jobs and the few scarce dollars available. When we left, it was like parting from friends.

I hated leaving the peaceful country setting to get back on the interstate and rejoin the rat race. I could read the same thoughts on Marilyn's face. As we drove, our conversation was about different towns between where we were and Phoenix. Marilyn confided that she'd never been any farther west than Little Rock and no farther east than Nashville.

"Darryl used to talk about Houston and Tampa and St. Louis, but he made them all sound nasty and dangerous," my lovely friend told me. "He said that he'd never go to Chicago or Detroit because only the criminals carried guns. I watch the news and it's easy to see that murder rates go up in any big city."

"Dear," I said, "if you've never heard this before, listen up. Two percent of humans are psychotic. That means that they have no conscience and are capable of anything. Do the arithmetic. If the town we just left has five hundred people, statistically, it would also have ten psychotics. Most psychotics stick out like a sore thumb, especially in a little town like that. The psychotic with a high IQ is harder to detect and therefore more dangerous. It's easy to keep track of them in a small town. In big cities, there are so many that the police are overwhelmed. In a large metropolitan area like surrounds Houston, Chicago, or Los Angeles, there may be as many as a hundred thousand evil people running around. Two percent of that minority are incredibly smart to boot. That would make for two thousand seriously dangerous people. Can you imagine the problem in New York, London, or Tokyo? Darryl might not have had his finger exactly on the pulse, but he was right about avoiding big towns. Detroit, DC, and Chicago have reputations well earned. Unfortunately, the psychotics think they have to live up to those reputations."

"How many people are there in the Phoenix metropolitan area?" Marilyn asked.

I did the math in my head and told her that there would presumably be sixty thousand creeps with twelve hundred that would be hard to detect before I said, "Three million."

"Sugar, I'm from Chicago. I've lived in Phoenix, Houston and El Paso plus a few other smaller Hell-holes around the nation. I can smell a psycho a mile off. I can usually spot the smart ones by looking in their eyes. I've even sensed them in a room before I ever laid eyes on them. I once drove past one's house that gave me the creeps and I never met the man and didn't know that he lived there. When he died, I never got that feeling in his neck of the woods again. It's a gift from the Lord and I thank him for it. I spotted Slim for a psycho and stopped him in his tracks. You're pretty safe with me," I informed her, hoping to make her feel like she was both "safe" and "with" me.

"You're right about Slim, but he was dumb. Anyway, I think you killed him. Don't worry, I don't care. I'd be glad if you did. He raped me once and threatened to kill me if I told anyone. I was afraid that he'd hurt you or maybe even kill you. I started hollerin' right away hoping someone would call the cops. I was amazed and proud when you took him out so easily. Until that moment, I wouldn't have come with you. I'm afraid of tackling the world by myself, but I can see that I'm not by myself anymore. Darryl knew that Slim raped me and never said or did anything about it, not even when I told him that Slim threatened to kill me. He was as afraid of Slim as I was. When I called him a coward, he gave me a black eye."

I knew that what she'd told me was true and from her heart. Once again, I vowed to myself to never let her down. "I kind of suspected that I might have killed Slim. I was hoping to spare you anything so ugly, but the situation called for immediate action. Let's hope that he's still alive. Let's hope too, that Darryl will keep his mouth shut. I made Darryl a promise and I keep my promises." She didn't ask me what my promise had been. I think she knew what was going on.

"I know what that decal in your truck window with the blue rifle is," Marilyn said. "I had a regular customer at the restaurant who had a tattoo like that on his shoulder. He had an Eagle tattoo like your other decal on his other shoulder. He was the nicest man I ever met until you came along. You were in the 101st Airborne and you were in the Infantry. He told me what the infantry does. My friend with the tattoos died in a car wreck. He was hit by a train. He was always so sad. I always wondered if he did it on purpose to commit suicide. That was a long time ago, before I met Darryl. The man with the tattoos had artificial legs, but he walked fairly well. He never asked me out, but I could tell that he liked me. I think I was in love with him even though we never dated," she finished sadly.

She said that last with tears in her eyes, must have been smoke from a distant fire. I thought that right about now would be a good time to change the subject. "Would you like to cruise Houston on the way to Phoenix?"

"I would love to!" she said. "Oh, but isn't that out of the way? Are you sure we can afford the gas and extra driving time involved?" The little girl in her was coming out again.

My ruse worked. Now she had something happier to think about. "I can afford it in time *and* money if we don't stay too long. You'll like the countryside and people around there. There's a lot to do in Houston. They have a zoo, museums, and the Astrodome. Not too far off, there's Galveston and the Gulf of Mexico. I always felt at home in that neck of the woods, more so than I did in El Paso. Conroe was the best. I lived there twice," I told her, happy for her interest and eagerness. I think that she let go of her sadder thoughts just as eagerly. She didn't seem like the kind of person to live in depression. That was good, I like to deal in the present, using the past only for a learning tool.

Once again, conversation came easily. The miles disappeared beneath the truck's wheels. Eventually, she got sleepy. I dug a flannel shirt out from behind the seat for her to use as a blanket so she could crash awhile. I turned on the radio and found a news station. The world was no safer today than it ever was. It has always been God against Satan, period. What I needed to do was get near a computer to check out the news from the town where I met Marilyn as well as around that restaurant where I left those four men lying out back.

Sometimes, things have a way of sneaking up on a person and biting them on the butt. I don't want teeth marks on me anywhere.

Marilyn awoke when I shut off the engine at a gas station around three in the morning. "Where are we?" she asked sleepily as she sat up.

"We're in Huntsville, Texas mam. I had to mosey in here to gas up our limousine." She managed a smile for me.

"I have to use the restroom," she said, exiting the truck. That woman even looked good after sleeping in the seated position for hours. Her good nature and smile had a lot to do with her beauty.

"Look inside to see if it's empty, then wave to me so I know you'll be safe." I told her. She thanked me and did as I directed. I think she was surprised and happy that I cared so much.

"Lord, look after my friend when she's not near me," I prayed. Girls like her were jerk magnets because every man who saw her wanted her. I considered myself lucky that she even looked at me twice. She wasn't shallow like a lot of the good-looking women I'd met. I hope I never lose whatever it is that she sees in me.

Upon her return, I announced that it was my turn to use the lavatory. "Lock the doors while I'm gone." I heard the locks click after I got out. She'd seen enough of the rough side of life to be careful. If I had to guess, I'd bet that she was estimating the number of psychotics in the area.

I'd chosen to stay on the interstate, rather than trying to cut off miles and go through Lufkin out of Texarkana. We got back on I-45 to finish this leg of our adventure. I was really enjoying her company. Even when she was asleep, I felt better just being around her. It was like when she said that she didn't feel alone anymore. Neither did I.

We saw a black bear and several coyote before we got to Conroe at sunup. That was the first bear I ever saw in Texas. I saw a bobcat, a mountain lion, several armadillos, and a couple of alligators in the early and mid 1980's. I even saw a Red Wolf, which is an endangered species. I also caught copperheads, cottonmouths, rattlesnakes, and even a couple of coral snakes. This place was a zoo without cages.

Being a nature lover, this neck of the woods was like heaven to me. About the people, they could help you or hurt you, but usually it was your call. If you treated them with respect, everything was cool. Otherwise, you might wind up as an anthill in a swamp somewhere. Of course, like everywhere, you had to beware the slick operators.

Marilyn was staring out the window like a little kid. I think the dense woods and wildlife had her imagination working overtime. I could tell that she was enjoying herself and I was happy to be the one providing the good time for her.

"Hey Darlin'," (that's what the lovers in Texas call their sweethearts) "Do you want to check into a motel and freshen up before breakfast, or should we knock 'em dead with our disheveled selves?" I joked.

"This early on a Sunday all we'll run into are last night's drunks. You forget, I *am* a waitress. We'll fit right in wearing last night's clothes. If we got spiffed up, the crowd would think we were putting on airs," informed my gorgeous companion. "The church goers will eat at home. They won't show up until lunch time."

So I drove to a favorite restaurant of mine on the south end of town near where the old outdoor theater had been. That theater was in ruin before I moved to town in 1982. It was a great place to hunt for snakes though. As far as that goes, when the river was high, the streets in town are a great place to find snakes!

Everything looked way different from the Conroe I lived in twenty years ago. At least the eatery was still in business. It was one of two restaurants in town that the cops went to. The other was near the interstate on FM 105. I preferred this one on Frazier Street because of the memories.

We were among the first to show up. There was a big County Cop at the counter getting his thermos filled with coffee. He wasn't as big as Slim, but he was definitely big enough to be dangerous. When he got up to leave, he looked at us on his way out. He nodded at me, but he didn't smile. Hey, the man was a cop. They have tough jobs. He was doing his.

Without looking obvious, I watched him call in our Wisconsin license plates over the radio. I held my breath as I waited for him to pull out. Marilyn was watching and waiting too. Eventually he drove away. I expected him to pull us over later to see if my ID matched the plates.

"Marilyn, that cop headed north into town. I think we should go straight to Houston after breakfast and get a room there or at least nearby. I know he will pull us over if he sees our truck again," I told her.

"You're right dear. I could feel that something was on his mind and

I think we were that something. Let's leave now. I'll tell our waitress to make our order to go," Marilyn said, getting up as she spoke.

"Excellent idea Darlin'," I told her, trying to make things seem a little lighter. I got up to pay at the cash register to speed things up even more. In a few minutes, we were in the truck looking to pull out on Frazier Street. Then I remembered Gladstell Street. The cop could have gone west on Gladstell and circled around to our south. My truck had Wisconsin plates. He'd gamble that we were still going south. I was probably being too paranoid, but I headed for Foster Drive and went east thinking to take Porter Highway, using back roads to Houston.

"Marilyn, I think we'd better take the time to pick up a newspaper. There's a little store on Seventh Street we can stop at," I said. "I have a bad feeling that our reputation preceded us." She made no reply. I could tell that she was worried. For the first time in a long time, I was worried too.

We weren't in the headlines, but we were mentioned on the front page. We bought two newspapers so we could each scan. When I turned to the page with the related story, there was a photo of my sweetheart above the story.

**Missing Woman Wanted For Questioning:** Arkansas resident Marilyn DuPree sought by FBI for questioning in a homicide. She was last seen with a blonde haired man in his early thirties, 6'1", weighing approximately 220lbs. with a chubby build. The blonde haired man is the prime suspect in the murder of William 'Slim' Bogseth. The pair is believed to be traveling the interstates. The man is also a suspect in the brutal slaying of four restaurant patrons.... The story confirmed my fears.

The article had babbled on about no witnesses in the slaying of the men at the restaurant, which was great news as was the description given of me. Darryl didn't want a closed casket funeral before his time. He was a smart man. So, I had to ditch the truck and Marilyn would need a disguise. On our side was the fact that the paper just came out. The cop was on the ball and recognized Marilyn from the photo, which was only a few years old. He was thrown off because she was with short, trim, brown haired Evan Mullen. Good thing I kept my real name from you. (Yeah, I'm still here.)

"Marilyn darling, there is a black, hooded sweatshirt behind the seat that's pretty clean. Why don't you pull it on over your blouse and put my sunglasses on. Wear it with the hood up. I have to call some friends to ditch this truck and get us some new wheels. We might get out of this alright after all." I got no argument from her. She did as I asked knowing that time was short. "Wait in the truck please while I make the calls."

My old acquaintance, 'Do Dad' would give me a couple hundred for my truck and White Roach would have a good running replacement. All of this hinged on two things. First, were these men still alive, and third (another crummy joke), were they in jail or still in the business?

. . .

Oh thank God for bad company. I asked for five bills from Do Dad and got two hundred and fifty dollars for my truck. I kept it in good shape. It was worth two K and we both knew it. I was desperate. Those are the only kind of people who go to Do Dad. He knows it and makes good money performing the services that he does while keeping his mouth shut. Still, it was best that he hadn't seen Marilyn without her disguise. All he ever knew me as was 'Snake Man' and the only name he ever gave me was 'Do Dad'. We both operated under the premise that if you don't know a man's name, you can't tell it to anyone.

White Roach had done time in Navasota as a youngster while his big brother had received thirty years for the same crime only as a repeat offender. Thirty years is what they give you if you won't make a business deal with the cops who shared with the judges and lawyers, and if you won't rat out your friends. Roach was a kid and it was his first offense when he was busted. He managed to stay straight since 1985. He told me once, "There's no broads in prison, just punks." I was glad to hear that he wasn't gay 'cause he was one big scary hillbilly.

Roach's ex-wife had dumped the man she ran off with when Roach got busted. She had come back when her big mean hillbilly got out of Navasota. She cut Marilyn's hair and dyed it auburn or some such color. It looked reddish brown to me. She was still beautiful, which was more than I could say for my five hundred dollar beater pick up truck. Roach was a mechanic supreme, bikes or caged wheels. The heater, radio, and all the lights worked *and* my crummy looking truck with the primered driver side door ran like a raped ape with its finely tuned 454 cubic inch engine. I understood that Roach had given me a deal and I figured that sometime down the road, I'd repay his kindness.

We still used Porter Highway when we left. No sense tempting fate. Besides, I had a friend out this way that had connections for paperwork and legal documents. Some folks only knew him as "Papers" which was his street name. It was past noon now. We still hadn't eaten our carry out breakfast. With our stressful metamorphosis taken care of, we could relax a little.

"I'm starving honey. Could we pull over somewhere and eat our breakfast before it goes bad?" asked Tina. (That's the street name she picked for herself) "I hate to waste food." Once again, she had a good idea. I don't mind capitalizing on a good idea even if it isn't mine.

We were near Grangerland now. "How would you like to meet my friend Newton?" I asked Tina. (Get used to that name from now on. Hey, she picked it.)

"Is he related to Fig Newton?" asked Tina, obviously less stressed out now.

"Darned if I know, Darlin', but he might be. The good news is that if he's still living in the same place, we can camp out there until he comes home from work. He can probably get some ID's made for you with Tina "Mullen" for a new handle. We're gonna need plates for this truck too. You can pretend that you're my wife. You could do worse," I said teasingly. "This guys nick name is Papers. Everyone thinks it's for rolling papers, but he doesn't even get high. He sure likes beer though."

"Do worse? Worse than you? Only if I really tried," laughed Tina. "Tina Renee Mullen, I like it," she said. "Can this Newton person make a birth certificate for me too? I'd like to be ten years younger, even if it is only on paper."

"My friend, Papers can make you an honorable discharge from any branch of service, a college diploma, or a demolition card. Today's computers and printers open a world of possibilities. You do realize that you sacrifice your social security retirement benefits by staying with me and changing your name don't you?" I said.

"( )", she called me by my name, "That would be a small price to pay to be with you," declared Tina. She must have meant it too 'cause here she was.

"Tina, Darling, forget my name. Start calling me Evan from now on. I'll get papered in that name. We can get a full set of documents including a Marriage Certificate. I'll be broke when he's through with me though," I informed her.

"You still have five hundred dollars," she said, digging it out of her purse and giving it back. "Remember, I still have money of my own too."

"Thank you," I said. "I'll gladly take this back. I'm gonna have to hit the ground running when we get to Arizona. It's a good thing I know people there too. We'll be fine. I can find work the first day we arrive. We make a good team. I think we were supposed to hook up when we did."

I said that last as I was turning off Porter Highway onto a dirt road, which wended through the ancient woods. Trailers and shacks were all that a person would find in this part of the sticks. The folks out here were respectful of their neighbors. Everyone had "dogs". That's plural for more than one dog. Everyone had gun(s) too. Actually, I always liked it out here.

His name was still on the mailbox. We had nearly two hours to kill before my friend Newton would be arriving, more if he worked overtime. Papers, I mean Newton, never locked his door simply because his dogs would eat anyone who tried to get inside. His first dog Sam died and was buried in this yard somewhere. The two barking inside his house now sounded like elephants. I had never met these new dogs that he'd written about a while back.

Tina and I got back in the truck so the dogs wouldn't come crashing through a window. I didn't have a gun on me and I was no fool. We made small talk at first, then whoopee in the cramped cab. You would too if you saw this woman. We still needed showers, more so now. This is what it's like to be desperate. I'd been here before, just not for a good many years. I'm sure all this was a new experience to my Tina, but she wasn't backing away one bit. This girl could go with the flow. She had been wasted and underestimated most of her adult life, I was sure of that. I guess she hadn't been exposed to very many opportunities along the way. It worked out better for me. She was a once in a lifetime woman. We decided to nap away the time until Newton showed up.

・ ・ ・

The dogs woke us up. We were still alone in the driveway, but I figured that their keen ears recognized the sound of whatever vehicle he was driving as soon as it left Porter Highway. His old Mercury pulled in shortly. I couldn't believe it still ran. It was a fugitive from a bone yard when I met him twenty-six years ago. I guess cars are worth fixing as long as they don't rust out like they do in Wisconsin. Road salt has turned many a fine vehicle into junk in short order back there.

The sun was in my face. Windshield glare prevented Papers from recognizing me. He wasn't smiling when he got out of his car. He never looked at my truck again. He went straight to his door and let the dogs out. When he came out, he was holding a shotgun. I was already nervous about the Canary Island Cattle Dogs running around. They looked like they snacked on Pit Bulls. We were what you called "treed" sitting here in the truck. I'm glad we backed off his house and waited in the truck. His dogs didn't need a window to crash through. These monsters could crash through a wall.

Newton's laugh got my attention. He was holding the shotgun in one hand now. I think he had finally recognized me, even with the passage of over twenty years. "Why don't ya get out of that truck and pet my dogs, man?" He was taunting me now.

"Call the damn things off!" I shouted. He always carried a joke too far. That was the only thing I didn't like about him.

"SHUT UP!" he hollered. Instantly, they got quiet. Now they were puppies again. Newton loved dogs. He didn't seem to have a mean bone in his tree-trunk body unless someone was stupid enough to make him mad. His giant killer dogs seemed docile, but they still looked menacing. As quiet as they were, they were still on guard, watching the truck. I went to open the door and they both started barking ferociously again, so much for being puppies.

Tina whispered, "I have some pepper spray."

I would have to tell her about my old dog Buster and pepper spray some time soon. Right now, I was getting angry with Newton and his beasts.

"Newton, damn you! If you don't do something with those monsters, I'll run the bastards over!" I shouted over the cacophony of barking and growling.

Newton had seen me lose it once and I guess it never occurred to him to use the shotgun on his old friend. He was more worried about me running his doggies over.

**"Juicer! Too Much! Knock it off! Go lay down!"** he yelled at the animals.

Cool names. I knew the jerks he named them after. Both of those men had been executed for rape and murder when I lived here way back when. That had been a real pair. I'm not perfect, but those two should have been drowned as children. His dogs grudgingly trotted off to what must have been pre- designated spots on either side of the front door. They were still looking like they'd rather kill me than anything.

"Newton, I refuse to get out of the truck with those two staring at me like I'm a piece of raw meat," I told him seriously. "If you can't chain those two up somewhere out of sight, I'm out of here."

Newton must have been lonesome and glad to see me, because he took the dogs inside and came out a few minutes later without the shotgun. We used to be neighbors and we were still friends, exchanging an occasional letter or phone call.

"Sorry, man. I never get any company out here. Juicer and Too Much don't know anybody but me. Most of my business is done over the internet and telephone through people I know for people I *don't* know. You all are my first visitors since I got these two cattle dogs," said Newton apologetically. "I need them out here 'cause I'm gone so much. They'd be cool if they knew you. They sleep with me. They think I'm their Daddy. Besides, if either one ever so much as growled at me, they'd get this." He fished a snub nosed .44 Special out of his pocket. "I'm no fool. I've heard of this kind of dog turning on people. I love my doggies, but I don't want to die like *that*."

His speech made me feel a lot better and his cannon made me feel safer. "Newton, I was passing through on my way between adventures and my life kind of went south, way south. My lady friend and I both need to be someone else. It sounds like you're still in the business. We need a full set of documents for each of us," I told him as I got out of the truck, finally shaking his hand. He grabbed me in a bear hug right after we shook hands.

"Newton, this is my partner, Tina," I said by way of introduction. Tina got out now, holding her pepper spray.

"God she's beautiful!" was all Newton could manage. He was under her spell. Me too.

It was time to tell her. I could see Newton looking at the tiny spray canister with a grin. "Tina, I had a dog once that picked up a dead raccoon I'd just shot. The animal had already been fairly well saturated with that stuff. He shook the 'coon like a rat, then dropped it. After licking his lips in disgust, he picked it up again and shook it some more. His nose was buried in that 'coon's fur both times. I saw a newsreel of a biker who volunteered to be sprayed with that stuff. He charged the man spraying him, wrestled him down and took the spray away. That stuff doesn't always work. There are some dogs and people that get mad when they get hurt. I'm that way myself. That spray might work on poodles, but I think Newton's dogs might look at pepper spray as flavoring on the meal they would make of you."

Behind me, Newton startled me by laughing out loud. I guess he agreed with my evaluation. She had a false sense of security in the form of that tiny spray dispenser. I had a feeling that spraying Newton would be a waste of time too. It was better that she found this out now instead of finding out on the wrong dog or man. Tina seemed to take it well even if she was a little surprised by the news. "As I was saying, Tina, this is Newton, AKA Papers. Newton, this is Tina."

"Papers, you've never asked me any questions and this isn't the time to start. I know you always thought of me as mainly a law-abiding citizen, and mainly I am, but I really do need to use your talents. We have a wish list and names picked out already. I can't afford an entire history yet, but we need the basic stuff pronto. When can we get started?" I asked my large, bearded, swarthy, and wild haired friend.

Yes, that was an accurate description of James Newton. He was actually an intellectual, more or less like myself, but he had an extreme mistrust and dislike for authority.

This big scary looking ape had probably been a straight 'A' student as a child in Port Aransas. Somewhere in between then and now, he became bitter. A crooked police force or a crooked town will do that to a man. We spotted each other's similarities in a most unlikely setting. I moved across the courtyard from him in a rat and roach infested motel that was so run down, it was only good for weekly rentals to us poor folks. We wound up as friends. His first dog, Sam, used to jump on flicked cigarettes and scratch them out with his paws. He would go after a lit firecracker too. Anything that burned or sparked became a target of Sam's wrath. Newton was the only one who could pet him. He never went after anyone. You just couldn't reach your hand out to him.

"What do you mean, you can't afford a history to go with the papers?" Newton asked. "Your freaking money is no good here man! Don't insult me by offering money man!"

"Newton, I know you ain't rich. I expect to pay," I told him.

"Yeah, man? Well, if you want to pay, you'll have to go somewhere else man, 'cause I won't take your money! **Man!**" Newton made it sound final. This dude was my friend, "man"! I loved to hear him copy that old Tommy Chong personality. The character could have been modeled after Newton.

"Newton, I'll just have to make it up to you some day," is what I told him.

"Hey, man, I owe you," said Newton. "You scared off Juicer when he was going to kick my ass. I was too drunk to fight and he would have hurt me bad. That dude was nuts, man. Nuts *and* mean!"

Tina spoke up, "I thought Juicer was one of the dogs."

Newton filled her in, "Thank your lucky stars you never met the real 'Juicer' and his partner 'Too Much' lady. Those guys were like Freddie Kreuger and the Predator. Too Much was mean as a rattler and always on methedrine. That son of a bitch was nuts *without* dope. I grew up with that bastard bully mother...pardon me Mam. Juicer, he drank whiskey straight, all-damn-day-long, and *never* got drunk. He went around barefoot too, walking on gravel like he couldn't even feel it. There's something scary about somebody who can do that. Alcohol kept him mean, but I never saw him stagger or heard him slur his words. I always thought he was the devil. He came from Chicago. The guy was as big as a house, way bigger than me. Bigger'n'shit! The dude was half a head taller than I am and fifty pounds heavier, maybe more. Anyway, they were slummin' and wound up over at the sleaze bag motel where ( ) and I used to live."

"Newton, forget you ever knew my name," I said. "My name is Evan Mullen. Memorize it in case anybody ever asks. If Do Dad asks if I stopped by, tell him no. I bought Roach's truck and Do Dad bought my old one."

"I recognized the truck. I couldn't figure out why his big old tattooed arm wasn't hanging out the window like it always is. I knew it wasn't him and his wife. That big mean hillbilly is a hell of a mechanic. He helped me put the new engine in my Mercury," said Newton. "He's cool. He'd die before he ratted you out. I don't talk to Do Dad any more. He was always in it for the money anyway. Besides, you put on

26

thirty pounds of muscle. You are hard to recognize. Even your face filled in."

"There was more work when I went up north," I informed him. "I started exercising again and eating. Hell, when you knew me, I was always undernourished. Yankees had a hard time finding work in those days."

Newton started again, "Back to my story, Tina. Juicer and Too Much came by our motel one Saturday night 'cause a bunch of us were outside drinkin' beer and playin' music. Your man, Evan, right? He was inside trying to sleep 'cause he had worked 'til dark and had a roof to finish the next morning. Too Much was getting loud and trying to start a fight with one of the Vietnamese guys that lived there. I told him to leave the little guy alone, which of course he didn't. I was pretty drunk and shoved Too Much so hard that he fell on his ass. He started yellin', "Get 'em Juicer." Juicer was coming after me when your man Evan came out the door with a handful of his pet snakes and threw them on the big bastard, sorry Mam. Juicer hates snakes and freaked out royal. That's right. Your old man collected snakes."

"Anyway, when Juicer ran off, Too Much left in their truck to chase him down. Too Much said he'd be back, but neither one showed up again. Not long after, they were arrested for rape and murder of some Mexican lady from town. She lived longer than they thought and identified them well enough for the cops to know who it was. DNA evidence made the rest easy. I won't tell you what all they did to that poor lady, but nightmares are made of that stuff Tina," he finished.

"You sure got that right." I said. "I'm so glad those two were executed. Too bad it wasn't soon enough to save that poor woman."

"They never got executed, man. They were released a couple of years ago. They were supposed to be executed, but they plea bargained to escape the death penalty by confessing a bunch of their other unsolved crimes the two of them had committed. They served twenty-five straight and they are O-U-T man!" Newton shocked me with that revelation. "Yeah, man, and the news gets worse. They ain't even on parole or nothin' and the two of them are back together *and* I found out that they're livin' in Cut 'n' Shoot right down the road. That's why I got the dogs. That's why I named them the way I did. If those two ever come around here and call each other, they call the dogs too.

Pretty neat, hah man? The cannon in my pocket is as much for them as it is for my killer dogs."

This horrible news changed everything. Papers' news flash was akin to saying that Hitler was still alive and building an army. "Newton, it's only a matter of time before you run into them. You haven't changed much and they're probably still mad. Creeps like those two don't like unfinished business. They hardly knew me at all and might not even recognize me. If you get Tina and I documented, wall to wall, I'll do you and the world a favor and make them disappear."

"Honey, what are you saying?" Tina asked incredulously.

This was something that had to be done and Tina had to understand why. It was time to let her know what those evil bastards did to that Mexican lady.

"Listen up Sugar," I started, "Those men are demons. They'll kill again and might have already. They'll kill Papers too if they run into him. Remember the Mexican lady? They gouged out her eyes, knocked out all her teeth, burned her with cigars, stabbed her a whole bunch of times, and cut her throat. That could have been anybody. It could happen to Newton or even you. She was still alive, barely, when the police found her less than half an hour later. Do you want that to happen to someone else?"

"OK! OK! You made your point!" Tina said angrily. "Remember, I was raped myself. I guess I was lucky it was Slim and not the two animals you all are talking about. I never thought I'd think of that day as anything but awful. After what you told me, I realize that I have no idea what awful is. I'm sure you're right. Where will we stay until this thing is over?" Tina seemed resigned to the situation.

I looked at Newton for an answer to that question. He grew up around here.

"I know just the place," he said. "It's real close too. You could walk there in a couple of minutes. My boss in the Woodlands owns a house at the end of this road."

"I thought we were *at* the end of this road," I said, more than a little confused.

"It used to be. I sold my boss some of my land to get cash for a new computer and a better printer," Papers informed me. "There ain't much to look at as far as roads go, but it's solid, hard ground and you can drive back there another half mile. C'mon man, I'll show you."

I followed his old Mercury in the truck. The ground was hard, flat, and solid. In about a minute of winding through trees, I could see a nice looking ranch home with a camouflage paint job covering it's fieldstone exterior. The roof was Mon Ray tiles colored to match. The practically invisible car path went on past the house.

"Wow! A bulletproof exterior with a fire proof roof! I'd be happy if this were mine!" I couldn't hide my amazement at this radically cool house. "How is it possible for us to stay here?"

"My boss has so much money and so many houses, that he rarely comes out here," Papers informed me. "Right now, he's in Australia, man. He's staying there until Christmas. Then he will go by his mother's in Colorado. He always calls before he comes out. He runs his business by computer. I'm the superintendent for his business in The Woodlands now man."

Newton went on, "You two can stay here until hell freezes over, unless he calls and says he's coming out. He lets me use the place as long as I keep it clean and no one does anything to make the cops come out here. I ain't gonna call the cops man, are you?"

All three of us laughed at this. It was perfect. We'd hear the dogs barking if someone came to Newton's house unless it was raining. "Newton, my friend, you are truly amazing! Tina and I will stay until Juicer and Too Much are food for the fire ants. Then I have to go Arizona."

"Are you gonna see your kids man?" he asked. "I remember them when they were in grade school. Your kids were *too* funny, man. Your daughter must be beautiful now. I'll bet that husky boy of yours got big too, man."

I wondered if Newton realized how many times he said man, man. (Just kidding, man!) I brought him up to date on my two oldest children and my stepdaughter whom he'd only seen when she was a baby while he was turning on the heat and electricity, lighting the pilots in the space heaters that were scattered throughout the house. Afterward, we used his car going back to his crib so he could take notes and create our new lives as Tina and Evan Mullen. We made friends with his dogs. Taking their cue from their happy and relaxed master, they accepted us like family. We decided that the less vehicle traffic across the carpet of pine needles between the houses, the better. We could walk back to the hidden house when Papers took our photographs and information.

. . .

Tina and I had showered and put on clean clothes after we unloaded the truck. I don't like being dirty any longer than I have to. I put on jeans, sneakers, and a black T-shirt. She was wearing faded jeans, sneakers, a sleeveless blouse, and my sunglasses. I read the sunglasses as more camouflage to add to her dyed and cut hair.

Papers had offered to take us out to eat at The Wharf in The Woodlands. I hadn't been there since I helped put the wood shakes on its roof when it was being built. Back then, it had been too expensive for me to hang around. Except for the crowds, I was looking forward to seeing the place again. I was hoping it wouldn't just be a sad trip down memory lane.

Newton's Mercury ran like a new car. Thank God he didn't drive as crazy as he used to, unless he was taking it easy for Tina and me. On the trip to the restaurant, I kept remarking that everything had changed so much. Newton kept replying, "Yeah, man," without smiling. I took it that he didn't like the new 'crowded look' either as we neared The Woodlands. Time marches on.

I let Papers lead the way and do all the talking. He was such an ominous looking dude that people gave us room. That was fine with me. I wanted to finish my chore in Cut 'n' Shoot and go to Arizona without drawing attention. Tina was so beautiful and Newton was so ugly that no one looked at me. That was another plus.

The big meal had been welcome but it made me tired. I was reminded of the exhausting trip down here and how little sleep I'd had lately. A man can't nap behind the wheel. Stress always made me tired too, until my adrenaline kicked things in the rear end. I had been through some scary stuff in Vietnam. My adrenaline had come out so many times that it must have found a short cut. It didn't take much to get me going.

On the way back to Grangerland, Newton and I formulated a tentative plan for dealing with Juicer and Too Much. I would be dropped off near their house tomorrow night and just wait in the nearby woods until they showed up if they weren't already home. Newton had walkie-talkies we could use to stay in contact. He had a cell phone, but only one. The walkie-talkies would serve the purpose. I would need a ride out of there as soon as I was through. He was confident that our documents would be ready before lunch and a history in the computers before supper. He said that he'd get license plates in my new name too. My gorgeous partner listened carefully, but she never said a word.

Tina and I turned in as soon as we got back. She looked as tired as I felt. I'm sure I looked worse since I hadn't had any sleep. We took a pass on romance by mutual agreement. It felt good to lie in a real bed again.

. . .

This morning, I did my exercises with a well-rested body while Tina showered. She put on some coffee for us. I fixed the bed before showering. When I came out to the breakfast bar in the kitchen, I was wearing woodland camouflage Battle Dress Uniform pants and a faded green tank top. That's a "wife beater" to some of you, or a "Dago T" to others, no offense to my Italian Uncle and my five cousins in Chicago. I had a BDU AKA Battle Dress Uniform shirt tied around my waist, again in camouflage. I was wearing my crummy hiking boots in case I had to get my feet wet. I had two knives on my belt plus a cheap .38 special revolver in my front pocket. I never carried it because of my temper, but I dug it out of my toolbox for the task at hand. I told both of my sons and knew for a fact that knives don't run out of bullets. Speaking of which, I had about twenty spare bullets stuffed into a rolled up green sock in the front pants pocket opposite the gun. Tina never said a word about the gun or how I was dressed. I'm sure she had her thoughts but she was keeping them to herself. It looked like she was accepting the necessary and inevitable.

"Honey, can we go to a store?" Tina asked. "We should pick up a little food. I don't mind cooking."

"And I don't mind doing dishes. Sounds like a good idea. I never argue with good ideas," I told her.

. . .

We shopped at the nearby convenience store. The prices were as high as I expected, but it was "convenient" like the name proclaimed. At least it wasn't crowded. My attire didn't get so much as a raised eyebrow from the purple haired girl at the counter with the pierced eyebrows and heavy mascara. Our individual fashion statements were at opposite ends of the spectrum. Had we been magnets, we would have repelled each other. She would have "just died" if she knew how much she and I had in common. The girl looked at Tina more than me. I hoped it was jealousy and not recognition. Kids like her never read a newspaper anyway. The poor thing had no idea how old and worn out her "look" was.

When we got back, Tina fixed sandwiches. We ate outside in the last of a beautiful morning. It was unseasonably warm. The air was still and humid. I was expecting a storm later. It would be a good night for prowlers. On a stormy night, most people won't bother to see what their dogs are barking at. Dogs always bark in bad weather like they're trying to scare away the storm to protect their master. Even if someone looks out a window, they can't see a thing. For what I had to do, the conditions would be perfect.

We made love, then watched the local news before watching national news for a full hour. There were no detailed reports concerning Tina and me. They did make honorable mention of our story, briefly flashing that old picture of a "Marilyn Dupree". Even the trained eye of a policeman would have difficulty connecting Tina to the photo on TV. When Newton finished working his clerical magic, we would be "Olly olly ocean FREE!"

We dozed off in each other's arms. I awoke with a start when I heard the Cattle Dogs roar out Newton's imminent arrival. The trees and the distance muffled their barking, but the noise stood out against the serenity of the woods. Until now, bird and insect noise had filled my sleep. I got up to use the bathroom. Tina was awake when I came out. The dogs were unmistakably louder like Papers had already let them out.

"I'm next," she said. "Do you mind if I shower first?"

"Not at all, Darlin', be my guest," I invited.

I was sure that Papers would use the walkie-talkies to announce his visit when he was through with the dogs. Here is where I make a confession. I was extremely nervous about facing Juicer. He was as big as Slim without the belly. I shared Newton's opinion about him being the devil. My job would be difficult to say the least if I was found out before I could deliver the Coup de Grace or whatever the hell the French called finishing someone off.

"( ) can you read me?" Newton said over the horn.

"Newton, forget you ever knew my real name, over," I admonished. God that's corny. I take that back. I do not admonish people, I tell them stuff. (Yeah, I'm still here. Hell, it's my story, ain't it "man"?)

"Sorry man," he came back. "I'm ready when you are, over."

Newton sounded like he missed us. I'm sure he was lonesome living out here alone.

"I'm gonna shower and we're gonna eat first. Do you want to join us for a bite, over?" I told him that stuff, no more admonishing, cross my heart.

"Hey, man, let's get some pizza, over." Newton's suggestion sounded good.

"OK, I'll buy tonight, over," I told him some more stuff. See? No more admonishing.

"Man, your money is no good! Remember?" (silence) "Oh, yeah, 'over' man." God that Newton was a hoot. More importantly, he was a good friend.

"Newton, I got my pride, You have to let me buy this time, over," more stuff from me to my buddy.

"Alright man, but I'll leave the tip, over," he made it sound final. He was too big to bully and I certainly didn't want to kill the guy.

"Deal," I told him. "I'll holler before we come down so you can put the dogs inside, over."

"Out, man," he wrapped it up. You know, the 'stuff' we were telling each other without admonishing.

After my shower, I put my "Rambo" outfit back on. Tina was pretty quiet. When we went outside, the air was pregnant with the oncoming storm. It was about half past four, but it almost looked like midnight. Thunder was rumbling in the southwest. It felt warmer now than when we ate our sandwiches outside earlier. Underneath the heavy black thunderheads, wispy gray clouds were racing in the opposite direction. A real doozy of a storm was whipping up.

"Maybe you should wait another day," Tina broke her silence. "The weather looks dangerous." As if to punctuate her speech, thunder cracked overhead and the sky lit up with sheet lightening.

"Tina, I couldn't have asked for a better night. They won't be able to hear a thing and the storm will hide the gunfire from any neighbors living nearby." I thought I had presented a very good argument.

She looked at me for a second and said, "I love you. I'm worried about you. I wish I hadn't said I wanted to see Houston. I'm really afraid. Please tell me you'll be alright." The concern in her voice touched my heart.

"Tina, look at me," I said. "When I go out that door, don't worry about me. Worry about the rest of the world. You are looking at a man who has been underneath wall to wall napalm. I used to walk point in Vietnam. That's the first man down the trail. The Lord may have brought me to this very place and time to rid the world of those two evil men. I'll be just fine."

I didn't doubt my words one bit. I was worried enough to be careful, but not really afraid. I was actually looking forward to tonight. I wasn't sure if I should be proud of wanting to murder two unsuspecting men. I still thought Newton was right about Juicer being the devil, or at least a demon. There was something really wrong with him. I don't think Too Much even appreciated that aspect in his partner. If he sensed what Newton and I did about his partner, then I was underestimating Too Much. That could be fatal. Too Much might be a demon himself.

With that happy thought on my mind, I picked up the handset. "Newton, can you read me, over?" There was a pause before unreadable static broke the squelch. "Newton, can you read me, over?" More static, but nothing I could understand.

"Tina, lets get in the truck and head to his house. He knows it was us trying to reach him. He'll be waiting. We'll stay in the truck until he comes outside." She put a sweater over her arm before we went out into the gloom. It had already started raining.

In the time it took to get to Newton's, the rain changed to a downpour, then suddenly stopped. Newton came out with a sober expression set on his face. He nodded toward his car and we all piled in as the sky broke open again. Before we reached Porter Road, the rain had stopped.

I said, "I'm sure I don't have to remind you two southerners that tornadoes are around when the rain starts and stops like this."

"This reminds me of when you were down here last time and that Hurricane was in the Gulf, man." Newton pronounced it "Guff" like is the norm around the Gulf of Mexico. "We had twelve tornadoes pass over Conroe. One tore up Panorama Village in Willis. Trees were down everywhere. You had a lot of roofing jobs then, man."

"You do realize that our walkie-talkies will be useless tonight," I said, stating the obvious. Just then, there was a blinding flash of lightening and another heart stopping clap of thunder scared the crap out of all of us. Lightening had hit something nearby from the sound of the explosion. The rain started again in earnest.

Newton was pumping the breaks to slow us to a stop. There was a huge Oak tree blocking most of the road. We couldn't drive around it if we wanted to. "We'll have to go back to Conroe, man, if we want pizza tonight." He kept the car on the pavement as he see-sawed the big Mercury around.

Through all this, Tina never said a word. Her silent mood made me feel guilty like I was leading her down dangerous paths from which there was no returning. I had to admit, that is exactly what was happening. Her bridges were burned when we fled her mobile home in Arkansas. Now, I was leading her into even more frightening territory.

Newton drove in silence, concentrating on the road in the blinding rain. When we turned onto Foster Drive, the rain was coming sideways out of the south. The wind would rock his car at every opening in the trees. Finally Tina spoke up.

"Do you think I could get a room in Conroe?" she asked. "I don't want to go to Cut 'n' Shoot with you all and I'm afraid to stay at the house in the woods alone."

"Tina, you've come up with the perfect solution. I should have thought of that myself. I'll leave you with most of the cash just in case something goes south." I was glad to hear her voice again.

"No you don't, mister. Hold on to that money. You are going to be fine and I'm going to make you happy for the rest of your life. Don't jinx this by saying something might happen because nothing will. I've been praying about us since I found out what had to be done. Just do what you have to do and come back to me in one piece," she ordered. She was definitely admonishing me, no doubt about it.

"Tina, I love you to pieces girl! I like what you just said, and how you said it. Still, it makes no sense for me to sneak around in the rain with most of our cash on me. It will just get wet if I hold onto it. I was going to have you hold my wallet and ID anyway. Speaking of which...."

Newton broke his silence, "Everything is ready, man. Tina Mullen, born in 1958 in Little Rock with a history the CIA would be proud of. You, Evan Mullen, are an old fart, born in Chicago, 1948, honorable discharge from the army. High school diploma from Lane Tech, associates degree in Modern Construction Technology from IIT in Crystal Lake, Illinois. You both already have Arizona driver's licenses with Phoenix addresses. Your homes were torn down to expand the freeway system and you're moving to Payson before you update your information. Tina has a Masters in fine arts from Arkansas State University, Little Rock. I made her smarter than you, man!"

"No *you* didn't, *man*," I joked. "The *Lord* made her smarter than me." Tina's laugh was welcome music to all of our ears. For a while, at least, we were able to take our minds off what Newton and I were about to do.

The rain was still coming down hard, but at least it wasn't blowing sideways anymore. The storm was drifting past. There were a few seconds between the flash of lightening and the rumble of thunder by the time we rolled into the Pizza Hut parking lot. The lights were on inside, but the lot was empty. The only three cars were parked in back near the kitchen door and were probably the employee's vehicles.

"Boy am I glad to see you all," the pretty young waitress said. "I thought no one was coming out in this weather."

"No one with any sense would," joked Tina.

"That's why we're here. No sense, no feeling," Newton finished.

"May we pick our own booth?" I asked the waitress. "I want to sit where I can see our car please. It's just a habit."

"Boy, you sure ain't from around here, are you mister?" The waitress was grinning when she said that. My accent stuck out like a sore thumb. I'd have to remember to keep my mouth shut. At least Tina sounded like the locals.

"Actually, I lived in this town before you were born Sugar," I told her. "I was forced to live in Wisconsin against my will, and finally made it home to the land I love. I picked up the accent during that unfortunate stay. Don't worry dear. I didn't pick up any bad habits or diseases while I was up there."

"Maybe you knew my Daddy," she suggested. "He's about your age. He was a carpenter."

"And what is your Daddy's name Sweetie?" I inquired nervously. Not everyone I'd met back then, or ever, for that matter, was my friend.

Before she could answer, a deafening clap of thunder exploded nearby accompanied by a blinding flash of lightening. As to be expected, the lights went out. Everybody jumped and the waitress squeaked out a little scream. It started pouring rain again.

"Move away from the windows," Newton ordered as he slid out of his side of the booth. It sounded like a very good idea to me.

The manager and the cook came to join us with one flashlight between them. It was one more than I had on me at any rate.

"When this rain lets up, I'm going to have to ask you all to leave," said the young manager. "This is the second time the lights went out tonight. I'm going to close and send everyone home after we call our carry out customers."

"We're all pretty hungry. Have you got anything ready to eat now? " I asked him hopefully.

"We got bread and salads if you want. I won't even charge you. Ya'all just help yourselves. Follow me," the manager offered. I thought he was pretty brave, considering how big Newton was and me being a stranger dressed rather peculiarly for a pizza parlor. Maybe he knew something I didn't. A lot of people had concealed carry weapons permits in Texas.

We ate our haphazard meal in the dim candlelight. I never found out who the waitress' daddy was. I was only mildly curious. Our next stop was a motel off Gladstell Street and the northbound feeder road along I-45. Tina checked in while we waited in the car. I gave her a hug and a kiss before Newton and I headed for Cut 'n' Shoot.

The rain was still coming down hard, but not so badly that we couldn't see to drive. We only had to go east a little ways out FM 105. I remembered that much. I hoped that Newton could point out the house in the dark. We didn't even make small talk now. Talking time was over. Our main problem once we split up, was lack of communication since the walkie-talkies weren't working in this electrical storm. We didn't have much of a plan, basically draw the two of them outside and shoot them. There were too many variables and unknowns to make a detailed plan. It sounds cold blooded, but killing them was the main goal.

Newton drove past their house and told me what he knew. The good news was that their home was pretty much off by itself. It was backed up to a flooded swamp set way back from the road on a long, muddy driveway in a low spot. The house had a few large trees overhanging the roof precariously. There was an empty field across the street that looked higher and dryer than the land their shack was built upon. Their house was probably used as servants' quarters once upon a time before some realty company divided the old farm and sold the better land to speculators. The nicer, but still modest homes were all uphill in both directions and more or less out of sight. There were a lot of woods between our quarry's house and their neighbors in any direction. I'd bet that they were going to get flooded tonight or tomorrow morning the way it was raining. They were on some very low ground. There was a truck in the driveway, but no lights were on inside. It was too early for them to be asleep.

"Newton, go past the house again with your lights off. I want to see something," I said. "I get the impression that their house is empty. It doesn't send out any vibes."

He went to the closest driveway and turned us around, killing the lights before we went back down the long hill. We stopped before the driveway. I took the bulb out of the interior dome light before getting out in the steady drizzle. Halfway down the driveway, I could see that the truck was on blocks. I peeked in its window to make sure it was empty before heading to the house. I knocked on the door loudly. By now, the gun was in my hand. I heard Newton driving away. Looking over my shoulder, I saw he had his lights back on. Another vehicle was coming down the hill from the direction of Highway FM 105 where Newton was headed. I could hear no signs of life from inside, not even so much as a dog. I ran around back and watched the vehicle approach. Of course it pulled into the driveway. I knew that Newton would be back, he just had to get out of sight to avoid tipping off the bad guys. Listen to me, referring to them as bad guys while I wait here in the dark to ambush them. It was kind of ironic, but compared to me these two were truly bad guys.

The vehicle turned out to be a flat black Ford Ranchero with a lift kit. It had one of those snapped on bed covers. The rumbling V-8 engine was probably a 390. It was more than enough horsepower for that light vehicle. I could tell by the bulk behind the wheel that Juicer was driving. When he got out, he looked even bigger and more menacing than I remembered. He'd shaved his head since I'd last seen him. Too Much was his wiry, skinny old self, except for being bald on top and his hair was gray. They both still looked fit, even for men in their late middle age. I steadied my pistol in both hands and first shot Juicer in the head, swinging my aim to shoot Too Much in the chest as I ran at him to finish him off. Both men were down. I was standing over Too Much with my revolver pointing at his head. He was looking at me calmly as I fired once more into his expressionless face. Turning, I walked to the other side of the Ranchero to shoot Juicer again. He was gone!

I hit him high in the face with a hollow point slug that knocked him back and down. I'd seen that much before swinging my attention to the other man. Terrified, I backed up in the direction of the house, squatting down to look under the car. Eerily, the Ranchero stood up on its front end and came tumbling over toward me. I fell to my right and rolled once, coming back to my feet. The car came crashing down where I had been only a millisecond ago.

Juicer was standing up where the car had been, facing in my direction. He was squinting at me through the one eye he had left.

"Snake Man! Welcome to Hell!" His voice was surprisingly calm, not even loud. I couldn't believe he remembered me and recognized me after all those years. Even harder to believe, he was still alive with half of his face blown away. I was so afraid, I almost forgot to shoot. All I could think was, "You can't kill the bogeyman."

He moved before I did, but no one can out run a bullet. Still, with another slug in his chest where a heart would have been in a normal person, he managed to fall on me, bowling me over. The gun was between us. I emptied it into his stomach. One of the rounds must have found his spine. He was just dead weight on me now.

It was a chore getting out from under his three hundred pound bulk. I kept praying that he was finally dead. Newton was there already to help drag him off me. The rain never stopped coming down, but it looked as if the storm had passed. I was drenched in blood and glad for the rain.

We flipped the Ranchero back on to its wheels. Too Much was not "too much" of a problem to get in the Ranchero. Juicer was a whole bunch harder. Newton dug the keys out of the giant's pocket and handed them to me.

With the cover snapped back over the bed of the mini pick up truck, it was time to get away from the scene of the crime.

Newton broke the silence, "Follow me in their car. I know a place to ditch their bodies. It's big enough for the Ranchero too."

Thank God the vehicle had a roll cage built inside. The windows were still intact. We got back out on 105 and headed west. I was pretty sure I knew where he was going. When we crossed the San Jacinto River Bridge, he turned down the fisherman's road going back north into the woods. I knew the catfish hole he was aiming for. I thought it was too obvious, but I trusted him. When he stopped, I got out and walked to his car. He got out and said, "Get in the passenger side of their car, man." He opened his trunk and dug out a long tow chain, laying it on top of the tarp that covered the bed of the Ranchero.

There wasn't much room to squeeze between the trees where he drove. I doubt if his Mercury would have made it. Sometimes the car we were in rubbed on both sides. I didn't know where he was going, but he seemed to. We started going uphill slightly. The tires spinning occasionally in the mud. Soon, he stopped. We got out and I saw that we were on the high bank of another bend in the river.

"I saw this place on a map I was checking out on the computer. It is supposed to be over thirty feet deep here in August, when the river is at its lowest. I checked it out on foot one day, so I knew a car could make it between the trees," Newton informed me. "The catfish here are awesome, man, way bigger than back there where everyone else fishes. I'll bet we're the only ones who know about this."

"Newton, I still have to dig six bullets out of these guys. The gun is registered to me. It's easier to get the bullets now than to try to account for the gun somewhere down the road. Besides, the gun was a gift from my father. I'll just pretend I'm cleaning a fish, or skinning a snake," I told him.

"I'll help, man. You've done all the dirty work so far, man," Newton volunteered.

When we found all six bullets, Newton retrieved the tow chain and we tied the bodies together, passing the chain through a bar in the roll cage after I kicked in the back window. We rolled down the side windows and pushed the Ranchero over the edge. It was about fifteen feet to the water. The car hit nose down and dropped like an anchor. We watched briefly, each lost in our own thoughts, before walking back to his Mercury in the gloomy darkness. We were both still bloody despite the rain. His car was full of blood too.

"Newton, I hope you realize that you'll have to torch your car to get rid of their blood and DNA," I told my friend.

"I was thinking that too, man" he said. "The old Mercury lasted a long time. I'm gonna miss the old girl. I'll just toss a railroad flare inside to burn it out. We can do it tonight so the smoke is hidden in the dark, the sooner, the better. When I can afford it, I'll get new seats and upholstery. White Roach can get it running again. Let's get back to my house."

Newton spoke as he drove, "What you did tonight probably saved a lot of lives, mine included. I think the Lord will forgive you. I can never repay you for this. I'm gonna miss you all when you leave for Arizona, man."

"Hey Brother Newton," I started, "You can always come to Arizona to visit. I think I should stay out of this area for a while. Tina and I already caught one cop's attention. What are you going to do for a vehicle?"

"My boss has an old Mercedes in pretty good shape. It's in the garage in that house in the woods where you and Tina are staying. I have the keys for it. He won't mind. The title is in the glove box. I'll scan it, delete his info, and print me a new one in my name. Hell, I forge documents for a living, man!" Newton's last statement made us both laugh. It pushed the night's grisly events to the back of our minds briefly.

We drove around back of the camouflaged house in the woods. Newton opened the trunk and took out the spare tire. We put four concrete blocks in the trunk and drove his car another fifty yards or so between the trees. We took the time to remove the tires, which were still fairly new, flopping them on the ground off to the side. Both of us stripped and tossed our clothes and shoes in the Mercury. He rolled his windows down and tossed in a flare, then we hobbled back toward the house. After his gas tank blew, we hurried back to the fire. Each of us rolled two tires back to the house.

I let him shower first. He had to wrap in a blanket. No way my clothes would fit him. After I was clean and dressed, I drove him back to his house so he could get some clothes and shoes. I was so glad I hadn't worn my jungle boots. It was time to go see Tina. She had to be worried sick.

. . .

After giving me a long hug, Tina demanded, "Tell me that it's over. Don't tell me anything else."

"It's over," I told her. She looked at Newton for confirmation. It was in his eyes. He appeared to be on the verge of tears. She gave Newton a hug too.

"This thing ends here, today. I don't ever want to talk about this again. I'm going to try to forget it and you all better do the same thing," Newton said.

"Agreed!" said Tina.

I just nodded my agreement. I had the most to lose if the story ever got around. It occurred to me, briefly, to kill Newton and eliminate a witness. I felt ashamed at such a horrible thought. Killing, no, murdering Juicer and Too Much had been a good thing as far as I was concerned. Harming one hair on Newton's head would be an atrocity. He was a kind hearted individual. I wasn't worried about Tina. She and I would grow old together, happily too. I'd share my grandchildren with her and she could share her attitude and wisdom with my children.

This is the part where I say we lived happily ever after, which will probably turn out to be true. Right now, it's too soon to tell.

Just remember, "The scariest thing on the face of the Earth is man!"

# COTTONMOUTH

Millard Crown hated his given name. It had been his unusually white teeth, large and perfect, that earned him his nickname 'Cottonmouth'. Most folks know that a Cottonmouth is a very nasty tempered poisonous snake. Cottonmouth, in all his young life had never displayed any of the traits of that evil creature. He wasn't a bully, though he was as big as a man when he was a youngster.

Cottonmouth called Freeport, Texas his home. He was a familiar person throughout the Houston and Galveston area since he went everywhere with his father during summer vacations from school. His dad used to advertise for construction cleanups and small welding jobs. His father was a full-blooded Cherokee who died while serving time for manslaughter. His half-English and half-Welsh mother had died giving birth to her only child, Cottonmouth.

Walking Bear, Cottonmouth's father, was the one to give him his nickname when the boy was seven and his teeth developed.

Walking Bear was a huge man but he was kind. His temper came out on a rare episode with alcohol. It was during this rare episode that a big cowboy in Houston tried unsuccessfully to whip Walking Bear who killed him unintentionally. The fool had thrown a sucker punch that was supposed to end the fight. The cowboy was too surprised to duck when his hay maker failed to have the desired effect. Walking Bear accidentally killed the barstool cowboy with his first punch. Naturally the big Cherokee was arrested. That was when Cottonmouth was fifteen. He dropped out of school and found work as an ironworker to keep up the payments on their little house in Freeport.

The ironworkers had proved to be a very rough bunch, quick to fight. Young Cottonmouth had been used to the gentle ways of his father. He had the instincts of a natural warrior just the same and proved it when the bully on the first job site got in his young, innocent looking face and shoved Cottonmouth. The lad never struck the bigger and older man. He wrestled the fool down in a violent blur of motion that actually scared the jerk for the first time in his life. What the bully had taken for baby fat had simply been undefined natural muscle. Cottonmouth had learned to work hard from his father and was a whole lot stronger than any of the other ironworkers had dreamed. Cottonmouth actually growled when he grappled with the bully. That fact was noticed by all, just as they all catalogued the animal speed and ferocity of the big half breed teenager's counterattack on the bully, a man that everyone else had been intimidated by. The bully never got the chance to use the martial arts he was so proud of. The fight was over before it had begun. That was the last time the youth was challenged. The foreman took notice and started teaching Cottonmouth more of the trade. The foreman had already admired the kid's absolute fearlessness at even the most dizzying heights.

Cottonmouth bought some used schoolbooks and studied hard to make his father proud. He intended to get his GED as soon as he felt that he could pass the test. He wasn't sure if he was college material but he figured that he might try night school as his next step. That seemed to be in the distant future as the challenge of his dangerous job and growing up dominated his present world.

. . .

Walking Bear had originally been sentenced to ten years with a chance at parole after he served six years. He wound up killing another man in a fight while still in prison. The guards beat the Cherokee giant to death trying to subdue him, at least that's what they said happened. Cottonmouth was the only person at his father's funeral. He claimed the body and took it home to Freeport where he cremated it on their property.

At sixteen, Cottonmouth was about as grown up as he could be. There was no insurance policy to pay off the land, so the lad grieved in stoic silence as he worked and studied, accepting his current lot in life.

Ironworkers were well paid, so he was able to make the mortgage and utilities with a little left over for the future. He knew that college wasn't cheap, not even in night school. He had been driving his father's old truck, keeping one eye out for the law, who actually were quite aware of the orphan's predicament and just let him pass. Now, at sixteen, he could get a hardship driver's license legally. Soon he would be a journeyman and the money would be better.

. . .

Young Cottonmouth was eighteen now with a high school diploma. He had gotten an accelerated promotion to Journeyman Ironworker and was told that he would be a foreman soon. He had a nice looking truck and had grown even more to six foot six and two hundred forty eight pounds without a speck of fat. He had never been in trouble with the law, not even for traffic offenses. He was watched fondly from a distance by the County Sheriffs, who thought of him as the well-mannered young giant. They all hoped that he would wind up on the force some day soon.

His career as a lawman unofficially began one hot day in July when Cottonmouth was in the right place at the right time for a woman named Clara Watts.

It was Friday and Cottonmouth's crew had gotten off work early due to a delay in a material shipment. This put him at his bank more than an hour earlier than the usual 3:45 PM. As he approached the door, it opened toward him from within. A man with a gun was backing out the door clutching a lady by the hair. She was carrying a cloth sack that bulged with paper money. The woman was sobbing, obviously terrified for her life.

Cottonmouth recognized the attractive woman in her late twenties, Clara, as a friend who always greeted him with a smile when he passed her by. He remembered her name from the sign on her desk. All this passed through his sharp mind in a tiny fraction of a second. He used the remainder of that second to react to the situation in front of him. His right hand shot forward. He grabbed the robber's gun hand in a vise-like grip, lifting it upward so violently that he nearly tore the man's finger off. The gun went off harmlessly into the sky. The money and thoughts of prison disappeared from the bandit's mind as his universe was swallowed by the world of pain inflicted to his hand.

Now in possession of the gun, Cottonmouth shoved the man to the sidewalk and told him to freeze. Writhing in agony was the best that the robber could do, but at least he wasn't trying to escape. Clara was amazed at how her fortune had changed so quickly. Her eyes were still streaming and she was shaking. Now Cottonmouth smiled at her, and it was like the sun coming out after a storm. At that moment, Clara became his for life. Sirens filled the air, and police cars rushed to the scene from all directions. The gun was still in Cottonmouth's hand and the arriving officers emerged from their cars with their weapons pointed at him.

Clara regained her composure. It only took a moment for the grateful woman to defuse the tension, since she was a familiar face to both patrolmen and detectives alike. The relief in the policemen's eyes was easily read. None of them had wanted to think that the quiet young man was a bank robber.

Cottonmouth handed the gun to a detective while the robber was secured and placed in the back of a squad car. Several other policemen were there now as well as a reporter and a cameraman. After a few minutes of talking to the reporter, Clara and Cottonmouth were asked to come to the station to make statements.

Clara rode in Cottonmouth's pickup truck as they followed the detective. She was a high school girl again, enamored with her rescuer.

Cottonmouth was thinking that he still hadn't cashed his check, yet very much aware of the warm gaze of his passenger. It wasn't wasted on him either. He knew that she was single and he'd thought of her more than once. The age difference never troubled him. He wasn't raised that way. Little did he know that Clara thought him much older than he actually was.

Cottonmouth enjoyed the respect he was given from the detective who questioned him and it made him feel at home. He didn't really have any friends, just the men he worked with. Not being a drinker, he didn't attend the bars like his coworkers who thought him odd for his abstinence. He never explained why he didn't drink, and the other ironworkers never pressed him for his reasons.

Cottonmouth didn't even know if he had a bad temper, and he didn't want to find out the hard way like his father had. Besides, he found women intriguing, and there would be none for him if he wound up in prison.

Now, here was an older man, and a cop at that, treating him like an equal. He felt that this man might become a friend. There was so much about life that the young hero hadn't figured out. With no parents, there had been no one to teach him.

When Cottonmouth drove Clara back to the bank, he had it in

his mind to call the number on the card that Detective Kohler had given him. He could use a friend and a mentor. He always thought of himself as a 'good guy' and it was easy for him to identify with the police. He was also contemplating the notion of Clara and himself being more than friends.

The ensuing thoughts had his brilliant smile straining at the corners of his mouth. He may have even been blushing but his summer tan wouldn't evidence the fact.

Clara finally broke the silence and said, "Thank you very much Mr. Crown."

This short sentence surprised the man. Two thoughts came to him. He and Clara had never exchanged names, and, she must have asked a teller about him to even know his last name. His intuition had never been wrong and he acted upon his thoughts by saying, "Won't you call me Cottonmouth?"

Of course that was a welcome invitation to the pretty woman who was getting signals from her own accurate intuition. They were immediately closer and bound together for life.

．．．

We have to go back in time to introduce this next character who you'll come to know as "Snap";

Anthony Michael Lazaro was a short yet sturdy little boy. He had been an easy target for bullies throughout grammar school. He was unhappy with himself for losing every fight he'd ever been in, as was his father, Michael Anthony Lazaro. Every single time Anthony came home with fresh bruises, his bully of a father, Big Tony, would take off his belt and strap the living hell out of the poor child. Big Tony told "*Little* Tony" that he would get a beating every time he came home beaten up until "*Little* Tony" started putting the bruises on the other boys. Anthony hated being called "*Little* Tony", emphasis on little, by his father *and* he hated being strapped for losing fights to all the other boys.

One day in eighth grade, not too many days before school let out for the summer, Anthony was in the playground, alone, as usual. A group of boys came strolling over. Anthony knew what to expect. Like clockwork, they started chiding him about his size. "Hey little boy, what grade are you in?" and "Does your Mommy know you're alone?"

Anthony could feel the terror welling up inside. His heart was pounding. One of the bigger boys in the group said, "I think it's my turn today." With no respect for Anthony's side of the fight, the big fourteen-year old moved to within striking range.

Something inside Anthony snapped. Not expecting any fight from the smaller boy, the bully was caught totally unaware. Little Tony leaped at the other boy's face with his hands outstretched like claws. His thumbs found the bully's eyes. Anthony went absolutely crazy on the bully's face. Blood was everywhere. Anthony was clawing and kicking and biting so ferociously that the bully could only back up, screaming. He fell down with Anthony on top still biting and clawing and punching. The other boys finally grasped the fact that their friend was in danger of dying at the hands of this little boy they had all thought so harmless. They grabbed Anthony, dragging the flailing child off their screaming friend only to find that they were now the object of the shorter boy's maniacal rage. All three of the other boys had to run away to save their own skins.

By now the first bully was lying in the fetal position. He was screaming, holding his hands over his face. Anthony was still in a rage and began kicking the bully in the head, trying his best to kill this punk who had tormented him for so long. He was lost in his attack when the principal, along with the security guard, dove on the now exhausted Anthony, pinning him to the ground. The nurse was called for. She sedated him.

It was determined that he had a nervous breakdown, and would be back to normal after a good nights sleep. The small boy did not get strapped that night. In fact, he never got strapped again.

Anthony was anything but "back to normal" and it showed. He gave off heat like a high wattage light bulb everywhere he went. The other kids shied away from him, even the few girls who used to be nice to him. Everyone knew that he had snapped. The boy that Anthony had savaged lost both of his eyes and there was talk of sending Anthony to a work farm.

On the last day of school, the friends of the boy who had lost his eyes decided to gang up on Little Tony and get revenge because they had lost stature the day they ran away from Anthony. So the three of them followed the unsuspecting boy at a distance as Anthony walked to his preferred isolated spot on the playground. All four of the boys were being watched from the schools office window by the principal, the counselor, and the security guard. The impending ambush on the unsuspecting boy was obvious to all watching. The three men hurried through the hall to the exit nearest the spot where Anthony always hung out alone. It was in the far corner of the baseball field walled in on two sides by a high, chain link fence.

The three bullies, bent on revenge, started running towards Anthony when they were sure their quarry was trapped in the corner. The security guard burst through the exit first followed closely by the other two men, all at a dead run now. They saw the three bigger boys jump on Anthony as a group, bowling him over with their combined weight.

Anthony snapped again.

Before the men could sprint across the field, Little Tony had fought his way to the top of the pile. The other boys were in a tangle with Anthony jumping up and down, trying to stomp them to death. All they could do was protect their heads.

From that day on, anyone speaking to or about Anthony referred to him as "Snap." He liked this much better than *Little* Tony.

. . .

The bigger boys spent their summer at the school in detention, grateful for the swift intervention of the three adults who had almost certainly saved their lives. Snap spent his summer and the next four years of his life at a work farm for delinquent boys. He retained the nickname 'Snap throughout reform school where he did manage to get his high school diploma after only one more fight. He won that one handily. The king of the school shoved Anthony and asked why he was called Snap. The king found out, much to the tough guy's chagrin.

Snap had spent all his free time in the gym, lifting weights, wrestling, and boxing. His sparring partners made sure that their headgear was strapped on firmly. He ate like a horse, gaining muscle that he never had, yet retaining his speed. He was, hands down, the toughest kid that that particular reform school had ever seen, even when they were in the old building.

On his eighteenth birthday, Snap was free to go home. His parents were notified but never came to pick him up. He'd only saved about six hundred dollars in his four years there. He decided that home was a good starting point, even if his folks didn't want him. Snap had grown into a very handsome young man, suntanned and generously muscled. He walked out of sight of the school with his suitcase swinging at his side. He was thinking about paying back his parents for never visiting or calling when a late model mini-van pulled off the road just in front of him.

He could smell her perfume before he got alongside. The woman's left arm was hanging out the door, her wedding band in plain sight. He looked at her face and nearly swooned. The woman was strikingly beautiful even though she was easily ten years older than Snap. He had never been with a woman, but it looked like that was about to change in a hurry. Her inviting smile told him everything as she said, "Hop in handsome."

Like all boys, Snap often thought about girls. What it would be like to kiss them and touch them. Then, at the reform school, some of the guards had sold pornographic magazines to the boys. All the pictures looked good to him. Every night, for four long years, he would think about getting out and being with a woman. As a kid, he pictured himself with girls his own age, kind of skinny but mysterious and desirable just the same. Then came the magazines. The women on the pages had delights that he only wondered about before. Now, he was about to embark on an adventure he had been dreaming about for a very long time.

The woman was a little on the plump side, which Snap found even sexier. Hell, what did he know anyway? She would be his first. They had driven down a dirt road to a creek that she evidently knew well. Without saying a word, she hopped out of the Van, disrobing on the way to the water. Snap was quick to join her.

It was obvious to her that Snap was inexperienced. She made the mistake of laughing. No matter how innocently she had meant the laughter, it enraged the beast in him and Snap flailed out at her. There was no one to hear her scream. Her pathetic attempts at fighting back were overwhelmed in a heartbeat with the violence of the attack. She was dead so quickly that Snap doubted his own savagery. The fact that she was dead didn't stop his desire. He had his way with her warm body time and again until he was exhausted.

When his passion had been quenched, Snap felt no revulsion and certainly nothing like remorse. His father had mistakenly told him as a child that God and Jesus were as phony as Santa Claus and the

Easter Bunny. He, being an atheist, had no feelings other than his own safety and gratification.

He was through with her and left her where she lay. Now his only thoughts were to clean up in the creek and get back on the road. At least he had transportation now. The seven hundred or so dollars in her purse were plucked out and the rest dumped in the creek. He was smart enough not to use credit cards, even if they were his own. Credit cards leave a paper trail.

. . .

Back to the present and our next character who we'll come to know as "Fum";

Fum awoke with a slight hangover. He didn't usually drink much. The woman in the motel bed with him looked only slightly familiar. She was badly beaten and her gag was still in place. She had a sexy body even though she was on the plain side. He had charmed her out of the tavern as easily as he had charmed dozens of women before. He really had no respect for women.

Fum was a giant, literally, at just over seven feet tall. He was blessed with an innocent smile that he practiced in front of a mirror sometimes. Women would call him ruggedly handsome. They found his good looks and charm irresistible. For a white man, he tanned well and he was generously muscled. He didn't have it in him to love anyone except himself. He was an only child and was used to being spoiled. He had his mother wrapped around his little finger as long as he could remember. When he was only twelve, he was taller and stronger than his wimp of a father. His mother used to drink up all the money that his dad gave her, not hiding the fact that she was cheating on her scrawny husband.

One night before his thirteenth birthday, his mother had come home a little tipsy. She had bought a twelve pack of beer with her. His father was away on business, as he so often was. The mother had given Fum a beer, then a few more. One thing led to another, and Fum found out the secrets of sex from his own mother. It didn't seem odd to him, only fun. They made a practice of doing this as often as possible from that day on, sometimes right under his father's very nose. His mother had finally found what she was looking for and never sought another man. Fum had everything and more that the tramp wanted anyway.

He was born John Richard Lacey, but was so big in kindergarten, that one of the girls recited, "Fe Fi Fo Fum…" word for word, from the story Jack and the Beanstalk. He was teased daily, listening to the fairy tale prose. It was the beginning of his general dislike for all people other than his mother. Eventually, the other kids got tired of saying the whole poem, and started calling him Fum instead of his real name of John. He liked it.

As his good looks and smile developed, he became the most popular boy in school, all the way through high school. Even teachers called him Fum. Now, at twenty-eight years old, he was still called Fum by all who knew him.

Fum had a mean streak that he hid well. He enjoyed inflicting pain. He was a subscriber to the axiom, "Don't shit where you eat!" So he would go out of town in his van, alone, seeking victims among strangers. His genius IQ made street smarts come easily. Things that other people pondered, and usually couldn't quite grasp, were easily understood by this evil and cunning giant. These mental and physical traits made Fum extremely dangerous. He got around to torture and murder by his twenty-first birthday. Now, after seven more years of practice, let's just say he was good at being evil. The poor, bruised woman in bed with him was living anyone's worst nightmare. He would kill her, only when he was done, much later.

. . .

Snap, was cruising casually down the back roads in the murdered woman's minivan. He was looking for opportunities, on a collision course with fate. He was about to meet his new partner in crime, unbeknownst to himself, and Fum, his partner to be. He was singing along to the radio as he drove. There was a full sized van alongside the deserted highway with what looked like a horse or something behind it. As he drew nearer, what he thought was a horse turned out to be the biggest man he'd ever seen. The giant was leaning against the back of the van with his arms folded. They were some awesome looking arms.

Fum hoped that the approaching minivan was driven by a woman. He was confident that his good looks and smile would make her stop. He was disappointed to see a thick-set young man behind the wheel. To his surprise, the dude was stopping. The man had arms like a blacksmith, but when he hopped out, the poor guy was only five and a half feet tall. Fum was wondering if this miniature gorilla had a gun when the little beast spoke up.

"Hey dude, what's the problem?" asked Snap.

Fum smiled a disarming smile and said, "I wasn't paying any mind to the gauge and simply ran out of gas." Fum was hoping that the scary looking little guy with the handsome face would get close enough to grab. Fum had no doubt that he could overpower the shorter man and steal his wheels, after he killed him.

Snap underestimated the big man's reach and was caught by surprise when the big dude lashed out with a lightning like jab.

Fum would have bet that no human could be that fast, and he'd have lost that bet. Snap ducked the jab and closed. Fum was seeing stars as the pain from his groin nearly made him black out. The little beast had him by the balls and was pounding his thigh with sledge-hammer blows trying to cause a muscle spasm to make the giant fall.

Fum was no stranger to pain, nor was he a sissy. He grew tired of the hurting the instant it had started. Fum grabbed this new monster by the throat, forcing the insanely frightening face back, and hissed through his gritted teeth, ""You let go and I will."

Snap had already snapped and was in no mood for surrender. The giant tightened the grip on the bull neck in his grasp with his huge hands. The shorter mans eyes started to bulge. Fum forgot his pain.

A light finally went on in Snap's head. He realized that he had met his better, and let go just before he passed out. The giant was good for his word and let go of Snap's throbbing neck. The big man was stronger than he looked if that was possible.

The strangers backed away from each other warily, then each one broke out in a big grin. For Fum, it was the first genuine smile on his face since he was too small to remember. Snap felt like he'd just made the first real friend of his life.

. . .

{Cottonmouth is the best one to tell his part of the story, and so he shall;}

I was quick to get Clara's phone number. She was what people called full figured. For this reason, I found her even more attractive. She was what I thought of as a fully grown woman. She was more appealing than the model type that most men seemed to prefer. Getting her phone number was something that I always thought that I might do, but was too shy in the past. Now, everything was changed.

Even though we'd never had so much as a conversation, I felt as if I had known this woman all my life. I was used to girls looking at me, but they were all common and too obvious. This woman was so much more. It was a wonder that she wasn't already married. She had even agreed to see me tonight for dinner and a movie afterwards. I was so overcome with feelings, new emotions for me. I felt protective and desired and energized all at once. It couldn't be love I was feeling, or could it? It must be, it was too overwhelming. These new emotions were even heavier than the sorrow of learning of my father's death. When I dropped Clara at the bank, I'd forgotten to cash my check. She reminded me. It was a humble reminder on her part. There was no sign of mockery in her voice, but she did smile so sweetly that I was awash with those new feelings again. That woman's smile could cost me my freedom. Would I call her tonight? You bet! Wild animals couldn't keep me away from her now.

Clara was in the shower when she answered the phone. I was flattered that my call should be so important to her. I wrote down her address and told her that I'd be there in about an hour. She lived a lot closer than I expected. I guess she didn't make too much at the bank and my neck of the woods was all that she could afford. Or, maybe, hopefully, she just liked living outside of town.

My shower was meticulous, my shave almost too close. I put on some blue jeans and a black rodeo shirt. The darn thing was my only decent shirt and it was pretty tight. Finding clothes to fit has always been a problem. I almost forgot the paper with her address on the counter. She wasn't the only one who was excited. I didn't have any dress shoes, but I needed to buy some new work boots, which I did on the way to the florists, wearing the new boots to Clara's. I was just over an hour getting to her small but homey cottage. When Clara opened the door, I let the flowers lead the way. Her smile told me I was forgiven for being a little late.

She always looked pretty at the bank, but I could tell that she'd taken extra care to look good for me. I gave out a big wolf whistle and she blushed, which made me smile. She never took her eyes off mine and smiled back. I was hypnotized. I don't think she knew her power over me. Yeah, this girl was the one.

She put the flowers in a vase and came back to take my arm and ask, "Shall we go?"

I didn't want to leave the cozy and cheerful little house, but I knew that if I stayed, my hormones might get me in trouble. God she was beautiful. I couldn't tell if her hair was brown or dark red. It changed with the light. Her skin was white and smooth, not a blemish in sight. It was like I was seeing the real Clara for the first time. She was the grown up version of Snow White.

We walked out to my truck, still arm in arm. The touch of her against me was having an effect that I hoped she wouldn't notice when I let go her arm and opened her door. If she noticed, she hid it well. However, when I climbed behind the wheel, she was blushing and just looking out the window. I hoped that I didn't make her uncomfortable. At least she didn't jump out and run back inside.

It was awfully quiet as I backed out of her driveway. I wasn't much for conversation, but right now, it was as if my throat was paralyzed. I couldn't even think of anything 'to' say if I *could* talk. I was having a hard time thinking at all.

I felt so awkward. I was sure that she'd think I was too young for her. I finally got the courage to look her way. She was looking at me with that sweet, soul stealing smile, which, of course, made me smile. We both laughed. Thank God! My throat wasn't paralyzed after all.

Our laughter had disarmed the moment and Clara spoke, "Would you mind if we call Detective Kohler from the restaurant? I went to school with his wife, Amanda. Sometimes the three of us go out together. Frank, that is detective Kohler, is a lot of fun when he's not working."

I was under her power and couldn't say "no" to her. I would have jumped into a lake of fire for this fascinating woman if she only hinted that that was what she wanted. "Sounds good to me. I thought the detective was a nice person. He was very respectful and polite, overall, a likable man. I'm old for my years and he didn't make me feel uncomfortable or anything."

"Oh no, Frank's not like that at all. He said more than once that he thought you'd make a good Policeman, maybe a detective some day. He likes you," said Clara encouragingly. "His wife, Amy, called. I told her about our date. She wants to meet you. She said that they had no plans and she'd run it by Frank."

The rest of the drive was filled with happy conversation. Clara was fun and easy to get along with. She was cheerful and had a good sense of humor. Although I never told her which restaurant we were going to, she didn't act surprised when we pulled into the parking lot of John's New Restaurant. I guess it was the only logical place on that end of town. The other places were too smoky and weren't as clean or brightly lit. I seldom ate out, but it didn't take long before I determined that John's was the best with the others way behind. The quality of the food was better. John's waitresses weren't a bit lazy or grumpy either.

When I opened the foyer door to John's, Clara went straight to the phone. I glanced around the restaurant as she dialed and spotted Detective Kohler sitting a few tables away with a petite little strawberry blonde that I assumed to be Amanda. He caught my eye and waved. I tapped Clara on the shoulder and clicked the receiver down. She looked to where I nodded my head and smiled to the other couple.

We entered the dining room and were immediately invited to join the Kohlers. Frank stood up and said, "Good to see you again Mr. Crown," as he shook my hand. He had the grip of a wrestler, but he didn't play any macho games by trying to squeeze too hard. For the record, I had never been beaten, ever, when anyone wanted to compete in such childish fashion. I told Frank to call me Cottonmouth since everyone else did. Amanda reached up her little hand from where she sat and said to call her Amy. She was looking into my face, trying to read my eyes. I guess she wanted to see if Clara had made a good choice or if I was just another shallow jerk out for a ride. She must have liked what she saw, because she broke into a friendly smile.

• • •

While Cottonmouth and his companions were dining in the outskirts of Freeport, evil was brewing on the Louisiana border just west of Beaumont. Snap had used the radiator overflow hose from the minivan to siphon the gas from that vehicle to Fum's larger van. Fum was amazed at Snap's ingenuity and said so. Snap said that it had been part of his alternate education at the reform school.

"You'll have to tell me all about it," said Fum, his eager mind always seeking new input.

They pushed the dead woman's vehicle deep into the woods. Fum tipped it over. They covered it with branches that the giant reached up and snapped off as easily as if they were toothpicks. Again Snap was impressed with the big man's strength, knowing in his heart that letting go of Fum's balls was the only reason he was still alive. When nothing shiny could be seen, they walked back to Fum's van. It was still light enough to drive without headlights as Snap gave directions to his parent's house. The parents who never called or visited in his four years at the reform school.

Fum killed the lights about ten thirty that night and turned off the engine, coasting up to the stucco house. It was the house where Snap grew up and was beaten in nearly every day of his young life while his mother watched. It was a big house on a secluded estate that was to make it easier for the evil partners to do their dirty work. Snap said that he would take care of his father and Fum could do as he wished with his mom, whom he referred to as "the bitch."

Fum realized that he had a vicious partner who could turn the devil loose on his own mother.

The mother grabbed the wrist of the hand clamped over her mouth and Fum lifted her one hundred forty pound body out of bed noiselessly with one hand. He felt the woman go limp and feared she might have had a heart attack. She wasn't too bad looking either. Fum was going to have some fun.

Snap had the gun from the nightstand and spun the cylinder of the revolver, dropping the heavy, .44 magnum bullets on the floor. Then he dropped the pistol. It was loud enough to wake the sleeping Mr. Lazaro who sat up, fumbling for a gun that wasn't there anymore, the gun he'd bought when he got the notice that his son was getting out.

"Who's there?" asked the shaking man in the semi dark. He didn't recognize the older, and very muscular teenager who was his son.

"It's me, Pop, Little Tony." Snap punched his father so hard that Big Tony fell out of bed. Fum saw that Snap had the situation under control. He turned his attention to the woman who had only fainted and was stirring. Snap's Mommy was going to wish that she 'had died' and Fum was going to enjoy that fact to the fullest, for as long as possible.

Snap, dragged his daddy to a chair in the corner of the bedroom by his hair. He broke the older man's nose, then hit it again. This time, he didn't snap. He was getting into the deliberate side of inflicting pain. Here was a new game he had found that he liked very much. He stood behind the chair holding his father in a head-lock, reaching around occasionally to punch old dad in the nose as they both watched Fum working on Mom. *Little* Tony had torn off *Big* Tony's eyelids, slowly, enjoying his dad's futile struggles.

Hours later, the unconscious couple was tied back to back and put on the bed. There was a lot of blood. Snap hit his father's nose again. The old bully's face had swollen so much that it looked like a pumpkin. The friends then took showers, throwing their clothes in the washing machine, and made themselves something to eat.

Clean and dressed the next morning, their bellies full of food, Snap and Fum went to visit mom and dad before they left.

"Damn it! My mother died from loss of blood," Snap swore as he doused his parents with gasoline. The cold liquid woke the father and he started thrashing and screaming. Snap wanted to hit him again but he thought it best to stay clean. Fum lit a match and tossed it on the bed. Snap had to jump back to avoid the flames.

Both men laughed. The mother started screaming and struggling too, much to the pair's delight. The poor woman had only been unconscious. Snap spit on her. The laughter stopped and both men watched as long as they could. When the heat got unbearable, they looked into each other's eyes and smiled, then went downstairs. Fum had the .44 along with all the ammo from the drawer of the night stand. Snap had never fired a gun and they held no fascination for him.

They walked out in the early morning sunshine as if they had just left a cinema. Their only emotion was regret that the fun was temporarily over for now. Snap's dad had a surprising amount of cash hidden where he hid all his valuables and secrets. "*Little* Tony" had found that hiding place long ago, but never took anything for fear of getting strapped again. He had visited the spot often, looking at his father's girly magazines. They were pretty tame compared to what the guards had in reform school.

The well-maintained van with the tinted windows started right up with a full tank of gas care of Big Tony's Cadillac. Our two villains left the driveway without being seen and headed off in a westerly direction, never dreaming that someday, soon, they would meet a certain Millard Crown, AKA Cottonmouth, or that they would rue that meeting.

. . .

After the movie, Cottonmouth said goodnight to his new friends and drove Clara home.

"Clara, will you see me again?" I asked, my heart pounding.

The wonderful woman said yes. Then she said, "It's awfully late and neither one of us have to work tomorrow. Why don't you spend the night?"

I started to open my mouth, unsure of what to say next when she quickly spoke again. "I know this is our first date and we haven't even kissed, but I think we both know that we were meant to be together. The Lord put you there today to save my life, and I've been watching you for so long, hoping you might see me as a woman."

She was right, plain and simple. Not wanting her to feel embarrassed or cheap, I did the best thing I could think of as quickly as possible. I hugged her long and tenderly. We went inside hand in hand.

It was my first time with a woman. Surprisingly, but obviously, it was her first time with a man. I was glad and vowed aloud that she would never know another man as long as I was alive. She told me that she liked that idea very much. It had been the most wonderful day of my life followed by the most wonderful night of my life and it was all because of the most wonderful woman in the world right here in my arms. It was on those happy thoughts that I fell asleep.

. . .

Snap and Fum continued on their evil path, wandering closer to Freeport via the lesser used roads. They were leaving a grisly trail of dead and sometimes mutilated bodies that was starting to get some notice. The first sign of their passing had been the woman's body at the motel. That was a total mystery since Fum had told the woman that he was married and would leave his van up the street as she checked in, hinting that he would see her often if their secret was kept. The woman said that she would be staying alone when she checked in, and the motel clerk had no reason to think otherwise. That was a minor display of the giant's intelligence. Fum's IQ was yet to be put to a real test. He had no police record. Until he did, he was an invisible man.

. . .

Snap was impulsive and only slightly above average in IQ. The belongings in his victim's purse washed under a bridge where some children were swimming as their parent's watched. The happy children gladly retrieved the papers at the adults' request. The purse showed up soon enough, pushed by the current, with driver's license and credit cards, all belonging to someone that the mother knew. She thought to gather the belongings and return them personally.

It was only a day later that her friend's ant and wasp covered body was found further up the creek by the turnaround. The prime suspect was one Anthony Lazaro, AKA "Snap", recently released from reform school. He was on the books. It didn't take long to make forensic connections to the youth. The fire department also discovered the bodies of Snap's obviously murdered parents in the undisguised arson fire of their home. Again, Anthony was immediately suspected and ultimately connected. An all points bulletin was broadcast for Tony Lazaro. The gruesome crimes were plastered on the front page of all the local newspapers, along with a recent photo of Little Tony Lazaro, AKA Snap. Fum read the newspaper, every day, no matter which town he was in. Of course he was furious, and worried, and wanted to kill the only living witness to one of his crimes. Remember, he had lit the match at Big Tony Lazaro's house. Fum had been careful enough to let his motel victim leave the bar well in advance of him. He'd actually let the cute little lady bartender think that she, herself might wind up with him. The bartender was sure to remember him, and the fact that he'd left alone. She had no reason to connect him to the dead woman at the nearby motel.

Fum contemplated the idea of murdering his partner in the future. It occurred to him that Snap would make the perfect scapegoat if things went south for them. He found that he didn't like that idea very much. Besides, Snap was way cool for a youngster, and the first friend Fum ever had. He was like a little brother and Fum felt responsible for the less mature but equally vicious man. Nah, he couldn't kill his buddy, at least not yet. Fum decided to keep Snap out of sight and told him why as convincingly as possible. All it took was showing the little monster the front page. Snap readily understood that he needed some sort of disguise and to stay out of sight. So, Snap would be allowed to continue his violent practices under the watchful eye of the genius-slash- giant called Fum.

Now the pair were once again in search of a target or targets of opportunity, drawing leisurely nearer to Freeport and Cottonmouth. Snap waited in back of the van when Fum went in the isolated little general store in search of some sunglasses and a hat. Those, and a baggy T-shirt to help hide his partners bulging muscles. The cashier was one of those busty country girls in her early twenties who was just starting to get fat. She caught Fum's eye right away. Pretending not to be too interested in her, Fum browsed around the store. The parking lot had been empty except for his van and an older model pickup truck. There was a back room to the little store. He was hoping that she was alone. He would make no moves if he thought there would be a witness. Placing the T-shirt and other items on the counter, he asked her if there was a restroom. Smiling, she pointed at the entrance to the back room. He ducked his head to enter and looked around before going into the tiny restroom.

The back room had been full of boxes with the rear exit barred from within. There was no sign of anyone else. He relieved himself and came out, now smiling broadly himself. He glanced around for cameras. Not seeing any, he walked behind the counter.

The cashier backed away from him, uncertain of his intentions. Fum simply took her in his huge, bear-like embrace, and kissed her full on the mouth. She struggled weakly, but it was obvious that he was doing exactly what she had fantasized. The poor woman wasn't very bright and lived her life vicariously through romance novels that she read to pass time between customers. To her, this was her destiny unfolding. To Fum, it was the opportunity he'd been looking for. "Why don't you freshen up a little. You could close the store for a while and we could go out to my van," Fum suggested. The woman was his and he knew it. She did exactly as she was asked. Fum emptied the register, including one fifty and several twenties from under the money tray. He was pocketing quarters when she came out of the restroom.

"What are you doing?" she asked. Fum told her that he was paying for the purchases. She didn't really care. All she wanted was some more kisses from the handsome hunk in front of her. They strolled out to the waiting van after she put up the "Out to Lunch" sign and locked up, all without a sign of a struggle. That was good. People would think that she left willingly with someone she knew.

Everything was falling into place better than he had dared to hope. He opened her door for her, buckling her in carefully, making sure to brush her teasingly. She was still responding favorably. He tossed the shirt and hat that he never paid for in the back and put on the sunglasses as he strutted around to his door, putting on a show for her. She ate it up. They drove away with the poor woman still unaware that Snap, the man who had discovered that he enjoyed inflicting pain to others, was hiding quietly in anticipation behind the curtain.

Fum's dad had committed suicide over a year ago, leaving a small fortune to his drunken slut of a wife. She had finally fallen prey to her drinking one week prior to Fum's horrible doings at the motel, but well after his first of many victims. Her liver had failed. Fum missed her a little since the pig had always bent over backwards to please him in bed. She was the reason that Fum simply had no respect, at all, for any woman. Still, she hadn't managed to drink up all the money and Fum would be getting everything as soon as the legal matters were taken care of. Hell, when he left her funeral, his only thought had been to kidnap and kill another woman. This poor woman in the passenger seat would soon find out that her destiny would not resemble anything that she had ever read in one of her romance novels. Not in any way, shape, or, form.

• • •

Bubba, and Duke were real winners. They had dropped their baby sister Sally at the general store, parking their old pickup truck, and walked back into the woods, hoping to poach a deer. They were too lazy to work, yet ambitious enough to sell venison, catfish, or whatever else they came across that would turn a profit.

Both over six feet tall, they were big boys by most standards, but the monster that they saw climbing into the strange van with Sally was the largest human either one had ever seen. Dressed in camouflage and standing in the shade of the woods motionless, they silently witnessed their sister willingly enter this giant's van like she'd known the brute all her life.

They decided to follow the van at a safe distance. Both men had killed before, but it was a secret kept between them. They knew everyone within many miles. Still that wasn't very many people. Yet, here was this strange giant driving off with their sister. They knew everyone that Sally knew, and that man wasn't in her small circle of acquaintances. Both of them knew for a long time that their little sister was borderline feeble. It was a miracle that she could read well enough to get through all those sugary romance novels. Before the van was out of sight along the straight stretch of county road, the brothers ran to their truck and sped off after the van.

Fum saw the flash of chrome as the truck pulled out of the general store that he had thought deserted. It could only be the old pickup that had been parked in the lot. The mystery of who was driving it must be solved soon. Meanwhile, until he dealt with that problem, he had to behave, since there was obviously at least one witness to his departure with the woman.

"What's your name gorgeous?" Fum asked the pretty young woman, flashing his practiced smile.

The girl beamed at the word gorgeous and replied, "Sally Ann Granger. My friends call me Sally. You can call me Sally too if you want to be my friend."

"Alright Sally Two," Fum teased, "I definitely want to be your friend." Again he smiled, putting his hand on her thigh.

The joke went right over the slow woman's head and she said, "No, just Sally, not Sally two."

Fum refrained from laughing out loud at this display of her lack of smarts. He had to be nice until he found out who was in the pickup truck behind them. "OK then, Sally it is. Sally, who would be following us in that old truck that was back at the store?"

"Oh God! That would be Bubba and Duke, my brothers. They went for a walk in the woods across the street. They do that every morning when they drop me off. They go looking to poach a deer. Oops! I probably shouldn't have said that. You won't tell anyone, will you? My brothers are awful mean and they might do something to me if I got them in any trouble. Please promise that you won't tell anyone and promise that you won't tell my brothers that I told you anything. Pretty please," Sally gasped it all in practically one breath.

Fum grasped right off that his passenger was terrified of her brothers. "Hey, Gorgeous, take a good look at me. You're with me now. You don't have to be afraid of anyone." He raised his left arm and flexed his bicep. The woman blinked in amazement. The handsome stranger's muscle was as big as a football. "Gosh mister! You're as strong as Herkaleeze!" Then she said, "That won't make any difference to my brothers. They got themselves guns. Lots of 'em. And they always have some with them."

That statement made it clear to Fum that he was indeed in a tricky situation. He'd outwitted everyone he'd ever run across so far. Even if Bubba and Duke were twice as smart as their sister, it still shouldn't be too difficult to gain the upper hand. Fum decided to get the formalities over. "Sally, dear, let me do the talking and just go along with whatever I say, OK?"

"Oh no mister. I can't lie to my brothers, they'd know right off that I was lyin' to 'em and they'd be awful mad at both of us. Besides, Jesus would cry if he heard me tell a lie. Momma used to say so all the time and I believe my poor old Momma, God rest her soul." Again, Sally was positively breathless from talking so fast.

Fum figured that this situation was going south real fast. He pulled into the first set of tire tracks leading into the woods and going God knows where. Duke and Bubba still thought that they hadn't been discovered. They got up to the little road to nowhere in particular and drove in after the van, which held their baby sister.

Fum was right. They were exactly twice as smart as their sister. Even combined, they were no match for the evil giant. Fum sped down the bumpy dirt road as it twisted around through the trees. "Snap, get up here and take this broad," Fum ordered as he jerked to a stop and unbuckled the woman. A knotted pair of hands reached from the back and dragged the petrified woman through the curtains. Fum grabbed the .44 magnum from the glove box and told Snap to make her scream. Scream she did as snap tore her clothes off, oblivious to the pair of good for nothings closing in on the party. Fum hopped out and stepped behind a tree before Duke and Bubba were close enough to hear their sister. When they did, they threw caution to the wind.

They nearly crashed into the van as they stopped on the pine needle strewn car path, leaping out with their rifles carelessly held in one hand.

The first boom from the .44 spit out a slug that hit the beefier Bubba in the spine just below his neck, sending him sprawling to the ground. The second boom was the end for Duke who had turned to face the noise. The slug caught him high in the chest and turned his camouflage shirt red. The impact slammed his wiry body against a tree. The smile on Fum's grinning face was the last thing old Duke expected to see. It was also the last thing he did see. The shots were so close together that Snap couldn't get out in time to aid his partner. He was glad to see the smiling giant still standing. The two big hillbillies were searched for money and their guns were put in the van with the now unconscious Sally. Her nude body was pulled out of the van and dropped on the ground. She sat up at this unceremonious jolt back to the present. As reality came to her eyes, she registered the fact that the two bloody corpses on the ground were her notorious brothers, the bad ass Granger Brothers she'd thought invincible.

Fum admired the large bruise appearing on the left side of her face. He liked the way it looked and told her so. If Sally didn't know that she was in trouble when the gnarly hands from nowhere dragged her in back and the vicious teenager tore off her clothes, Fum's words sure did the trick. She started sobbing and her bladder let go. Fum laughed and grabbed her by the hair.

Snap walked over to the terrified and whimpering girl, his face expressionless. Sally was sitting up now with Fum still right behind her, gripping her by her hair. She was trying to cover her self, but wasn't doing too well due to the vast amount of charms she had to hide.

"Get her to her feet big man," said Snap who was caught up in the moment. The bodies on the ground never given so much as a second glance. The Granger boys were ancient history. Sally was on the menu now. "Bitch, if you fight, I'll knock you out again. If you ever bite, I'll punch your teeth right down your throat. Now, drop your hands!" Sally got the message and a lot more, again and again, and none of it was in any of her romance novels.

Sally Granger was lucky. She wasn't tortured. She did, however, get shot in the head at close range with the .44 that could be traced to Big Tony Lazaro and therefore, connected to Snap. The evil pair once again stood in awe of each other's absolute disregard for a fellow human being's pain and fear. These two demons were meant to be a team.

It was almost dark and time for them to hit the road. Fum put the bodies in the bed of the pickup and had Snap drive the whole shooting match as far as the little car path went in the woods. Back here, the saplings were growing up between the tire tracks. Most people never came back this far. A sudden chasm loomed up in front. Snap shut off the truck and hopped out.

Fum stopped the van and walked up to where his buddy was standing. They both saw the bridge abutment at the same time. So, this dirt path used to go through. With the bridge collapsed and decayed in the creek below, the road didn't get used any more except for a place to dump the occasional unwanted couch or refrigerator. It was a natural to push the old truck over the bank. The woman's lighter body bounced out of the truck about halfway. She had been one sexy woman. Even in death, she managed to arouse the two of them. Both men wished that they had kept her alive for a few days at least. Their fantasies, as secret as they thought they were, were shared by each of the evil men and served to inspire them to find a new victim.

. . .

Cottonmouth awoke in Clara's bed to the smell of bacon. The blankets were on the floor. He smiled that famous smile.

It was so bright outside that I knew I had slept late. I was starving. The aroma from the kitchen was good to wake up to. I peeked out the door to see my wonderful Clara busily making breakfast wearing the tiniest little see through robe. It highlighted all that good stuff that kept me awake most of the night. I put on my briefs, greeting her cheerfully on my way to the bathroom.

"Clara, after we eat and shower and stuff, I'll do the dishes. You're not my slave." She tried to argue, but after all, I was bigger than she was. We couldn't seem to get enough of each other, but I was pretty sore and I guess she must have been sore too. Around two o'clock, hunger and exhaustion sent us back to the shower. I was too big to join her in the small tub. There would always be tonight.

I took her to John's New Restaurant for a late Saturday lunch. There was a surprising amount of people still hanging around, a few familiar faces. John himself came up to our table and addressed Clara. " Miss Watts, I hope you're having a nice day. Amy and Frank were here at noon and hung around until one-thirty. Amy left word for you two to get in touch with them when you came in."

After we ordered, Clara went to the foyer to use the phone. As I watched her, a full sized van with tinted windows pulled into the parking lot. The windows were closed so I couldn't see inside. My hackles were up already and I sensed that something truly evil was inside this vehicle. The van slowed to a stop right outside the door. I expected someone to get out, but it just sat there while Clara was on the phone. I got up quickly to join her.

As I walked over, the passenger window slid down to reveal a short man with a baseball cap and sunglasses. He was wearing a baggy T-shirt that couldn't hide his powerful forearms, which showed no sign of fat. I judged him to be about my age. He smiled and waved at Clara. It wasn't friendly. It was more of a menacing leer than a smile. The young man looked hauntingly familiar. When Clara saw the stranger smiling, she turned away, peering through the glass for me. She looked relieved to see me hurrying towards her. I got a brief glimpse of a dark hulk behind the wheel of the strange van before the window slid back up. The van pulled out instead of parking.

. . .

Samuel Bottoms and James Richardson had been working together for the FBI for years now. More years than either one liked to admit. Sam was a detective and James was the forensic expert. Both carried guns and both men were expert shots. It was unusual that two seasoned agents had never fired a shot in anger, yet this was the case for Sam and Jim.

They had just finished up at Big Tony Lazaro's house. That charnel house had been truly a nightmare. It was easily the worst crime either man had seen. The local cops seemed to think that it was an open and shut case with Big Tony's son being the only suspect. True, his DNA was everywhere, but so was the DNA of an unidentified man. Also, there was one partial footprint in the sand at the edge of the blacktop driveway that experts had determined to belong to someone in the neighborhood of seven feet tall and three hundred twenty-five pounds. None of the locals were near that size. They had put that data in the computer and nothing came back. The 18 year old called "Snap" by the warden of the reform school had taken on a partner who had no priors. Unclear tread marks made in the dust on the freshly black top driveway resembled tracks found near a motel where a horribly beaten and mutilated female body had been found. The tracks were far enough away not to seem connected, still they had been found on the shoulder of the highway in plain sight of the motel office.

A cute little lady bartender from a few miles distant to the motel remembered a handsome giant of a man who had come in alone and left alone much later. He had spent several minutes talking to the dead woman from the motel according to the bartender. She remembered him well and fondly, giving a very good description. Lights were going on in Sam's head. Too many coincidences usually meant it wasn't a coincidence. That had been the case for the last thirty some years of investigation. Sam decided to send inquiries about a seven-foot tall man to all the police departments within fifty miles of the motel, widening it as far as needed until someone said that they knew someone of those proportions. Sam thought to himself, "How many men that big can there be?"

Jim, the forensics agent had a hunch that they were looking for an aspiring or former NBA or NFL player, male Caucasian according to the DNA gleaned from the grisly arson/murder scene. He had found unaccounted for hair strands in the lint trap of the clothes dryer in the utility room at the Lazaro's. The firewall between the kitchen and garage preserved that bit of evidence very well.

Sam had equal respect for his partner's logical mind and went on a wild goose chase to fill in the time while he waited for local police input on a seven foot man within fifty miles of the motel. All this was going on as Cottonmouth memorized the license plate on the van with the tinted windows. Texas plates, FEFIFO 7, odd, but easy to remember.

. . .

Cottonmouth asked Clara not to hang up until he spoke to Frank. Shortly, she handed him the phone. After the small talk and plans for the four of them to get together, he recited the license plate and told of the strange incident, describing the ominous looking occupants of the van the best he could.

Clara and I drove to the Kohlers' house to play cards with plans of ordering pizza later. Detective Kohler was smiling broadly over his wife's diminutive form on his front porch when we arrived at his home.

After our initial greeting, Frank asked me to step into his office. I knew that I'd stumbled onto something with the van thing right away.

"That plate, FEFIFO7 is registered to a John Lacey who just happens to be seven feet and one half inches tall and three hundred twenty two pounds. Minutes ago, I got a fax stating that anyone with information on someone of those proportions to call Sam Bottoms of the FBI. A man fitting that description is a person of interest in two murder cases over on the Louisiana border. The passenger with the sunglasses in the van sounds like this fellow," said Frank, handing me yesterday's paper. There on the front page was the creep without the sunglasses or hat. Anthony Lazaro, AKA 'Snap', recently released from reform school, suspected in murdering his parents, and wanted for murder of a woman whose body was found only three miles from the school where the youth served four years as a juvenile offender.

I had barely glanced at yesterday's paper. I was so involved in my date with Clara that I had forgotten everything else. Frank interrupted my thoughts, "Get this, Cottonmouth. Snap is supposed to be traveling with an unidentified partner who is in the neighborhood of seven feet tall and over three hundred pounds. That information has deliberately been withheld from the press until we can get an ID and hopefully a fix on his vehicle. It sounds to me like we just did."

"Frank, that was the dark hulk in the drivers seat. Those two were right there at John's. Let's excuse our selves and go for a ride. Maybe we can run across them again," I suggested hopefully.

"Cottonmouth, I'll have to deputize you as what we call a 'dollar a year man'. You'll be official and you can carry a gun. Anthony Lazaro's father had a .44 magnum revolver registered to him that is unaccounted for. Either man could have it, not to mention the easy availability of guns in this state," said Frank.

Since all that I'd ever shot was a rifle, Frank loaned me his Winchester. It was a lever action one like the ones used in every cowboy movie ever made. His thirty-thirty was the twin of the one at my house. As big as I was, it resembled a kid's popgun in my hands anyway. I told Clara that Frank and I were going for a ride and maybe do some shooting. Amy got up and went in Frank's office to say goodbye.

"When will you be back dear?" Amy asked her husband.

"Call my cell phone when you get hungry and we'll pick up some pizza on the way back," he told her, kissing her on the cheek.

Clara acted disappointed, but I knew that she wanted to talk to Amanda alone for a while. We decided to take my truck in case we had to explore the back roads. Even if I was only a 'dollar a year man', I still felt like a lawman.

· · ·

Fum and Snap watched the truck pull out of the Kohlers' driveway and head out of the subdivision.

"Fum, you're a genius. It was like you said. That big guy at the restaurant made us and put the law on us. That guy he's with smells like a cop, and look at the car in his driveway. It's got more antennas than a ham radio station, cheap hubcaps too. Those dummies didn't even look our way when they pulled out. Can we go after the broads now? I'd like to try the little red head this time," Snap said to his big partner.

"Dude, you can rape the cops kids and pet goldfish, if he's got any, for all I care. I want that big Indian's old lady. That broad has *all* the trimmings. She reminds me of the one with those red necked brothers," Fum said to his honorary little brother agreeably.

The evil duo gave the pickup truck only enough time to round the bend before cruising slowly up the street to the detective's house. Too bad for all concerned, Frank neglected to call Sam Bottoms of the FBI with what he knew. He was underestimating the evil genius, Fum.

Fum dropped off the shorter, disguised member of the team, then drove around the block once. Snap walked along the property line looking up at the wires like he was a utility worker. Spotting the phone line, he approached the home from a blind angle. Then he pulled the wire out far enough to bite through it, cutting off access to 911 and help.

Clara and Amanda were sitting at the dining room table completely absorbed in conversation. There was a light but insistent knock at the front door. When Amy opened the door wide and friendly as was the custom in their neighborhood, there stood Fum, all seven feet one half inches, three hundred and (currently) twenty six pounds. After his size, Amy noticed his broad but artificial smile. "This man is no good," she thought to herself.

The little redhead backed up inadvertently from the menacing figure on her porch. The grinning giant used this opportunity to duck his head and quickly enter her parlor. He read the distaste and fear in her eyes. He knew that for once, a woman wasn't buying his smile.

"Clara, call 911," shouted Amy to her friend. Of course Clara couldn't get a dial tone. Amy made a dash towards the back door and ran into the arms of the leering Snap. He picked her up underneath one of his arms and clamped a powerful hand over her mouth before the little woman could utter a scream.

When Amy ran by, Clara dropped the useless phone and ran after her. She was caught from behind as a huge hand completely engulfed her face, threatening to smother her. She hadn't seen Fum yet, but the gargantuan hand cutting off her sight and air told her that she was in the grasp of someone larger even than Cottonmouth.

. . .

Agent Bottoms cell phone rang. The call informed him of a missing person, foul play suspected. What really got his attention was that a hidden security camera at the store where the woman was snatched from had shown a man well over seven feet tall with his boots on. He was wandering around, obviously looking for cameras. "Bingo!" thought Sam. He called his partner, Jim. Shortly, the two of them were headed in the wrong direction.

. . .

Cottonmouth and his new friend Frank were cruising around in the truck, which had no police radio, not even a CB. Detective Kohler's cell phone would never get a call for pizza or anything from his wife since Snap had taken care of that annoying possibility. Fum wasn't perfect, but the wire thing had been his idea too.

. . .

Snap had pinched Amy's nose while his hand was clamped over her mouth. He gave her sixty seconds just like Fum had told him to, even though she had passed out before that. The monstrous hand covering Clara's entire face soon had her unconscious as well. The less Fum was in the open the better. He instructed Snap to get the gun from the glove box and the duct tape from inside the console using the back door. "Don't run or do anything suspicious. But don't be slow either. We have to get out of here fast."

Snap did as he was told by the man whom he thought of as his big brother. Soon, the ladies were bound and helpless. Fum sent Snap to lug the dryer into the front room while he gutted the large upright freezer. Amy fit easily into the dryer. Clara was a tighter but delightful squeeze to fit in the freezer. Snap backed the van over the lawn as close to the porch as the bushes would allow. The two gorillas easily loaded their cargo in the back of the van. That had been a more difficult squeeze than putting Clara in the freezer. Both men were nervous and sweating profusely as they drove away as casually as they could appear. The back doors of the van had been tied shut with Snap's baggy T-shirt.

When they were out of the neighborhood, Fum sped up. Snap scurried in the back, ripping the door off the dryer and flipping open the freezer. He knew from experience that a woman who feared for her life was a whole lot more fun than one who was already dead. He hoped to take that secret to his grave.

Fum stayed on the main road, going back east where he assumed that no one would expect them to go. He was right.

They'd been driving around for three hours now without any luck. Frank decided to call home since he was hungry and hadn't heard from Amy. Of course he couldn't get through. The mechanical message said that the phone was temporarily out of service. "Cottonmouth, turn around, I think something's wrong at my house." They raced back to the Kohler residence with Cottonmouth leaning on the horn often. The detective cursed himself for not calling Agent Bottoms like he should have. He did that very thing now. He cursed himself again for not getting a German Shepherd like his wife had wanted. Frank couldn't know, but Fum used to say that he liked German Shepherds because they tasted like chicken.

. . .

I drove like a madman, thinking of Clara being in danger. I was praying as I drove that it would be a false alarm. The pickup almost rolled when I turned into Frank's subdivision. I slowed down just a little to avoid hitting some poor child. I pulled in and jammed it in park, leaving my truck running and the door open as I jumped out. Their front door was open and there were tire tracks on the lawn. My heart did a flip in my chest. I guess it was adrenaline in my veins 'cause I felt like superman. I could see better and every sound seemed to be magnified. I was breathing great volumes of air as I leaped the stairs and bounded through the house with Frank on my heels. The phone was lying on the floor. The kitchen floor was strewn with food and there was an open space on one wall where something was obviously missing. Frank and I were calling for the women when he stopped and said, "The freezer is gone!" The implications of that odd statement froze the blood in both of our veins.

Frank dialed 911 on his cell phone to order an APB for the full sized gray van with the license FEFIFO7. We split up and ran through the now vacant house. I saw that he had his gun out. I had left the rifle in the truck in my haste. He shouted from the attached garage that the dryer was missing too. Frank ran out the door hollering, "Get the rifle and come with me!"

I watched Frank juggle his radio as he backed out. It seemed that his car moved in slow motion. The unmarked squad had strobes on the front and rear dash and a deafening siren that filled the limits of my enhanced hearing painfully. My new friend was all cop now and it was comforting to watch him react to our emergency. He speed dialed someone on his cell phone and tossed it to me. He said, "You'll be talking to a Sam Bottoms from the FBI. Tell him what we know and keep him on the line."

． ． ．

Snap had ripped the duct tape gleefully from the women's mouths, threatening to knock them out if they made a sound. He feasted off the terror in their eyes. It was easy to lift the strawberry blonde out of the dryer since it was on its back. He stretched her bound body out across the dryer where he was spread out. He pulled the bigger woman to a sitting position. It was the best he could do for her now. She was crying. He loved every tear.

Fum had the air conditioner roaring cool air in the back and being wasted out the partially open back door. He had turned down the first dirt road that he saw. There had been only one house so far and he stopped about three blocks past it. He ran to the back of the van, fumbling with the T-shirt and finally just pulling it apart as he spread the doors open. He jerked the freezer out onto the road, bruising Clara in the process, grinning like a madman, yet in complete control. He tipped the helpless woman out in the middle of the road and literally flung the big freezer into the tall weeds.

Snap was quick to act. He snatched the little woman off the dryer and kicked it towards the back doors. Again, Fum flipped the dryer in the weeds as if it were made of cardboard. Both of them were running on adrenaline now just as Cottonmouth and Frank had been.

Clara was pitched into the van by the giant. He slammed the doors shut, closing her in the dark once more. She was getting claustrophobic all over again to add to her pain and fear. A small voice in her mind whispered that things were going to get much worse. The small voice was dead on.

Snap crawled up front to sit with his friend. Fum couldn't take a chance that the dirt road was a dead end and therefore a trap, so he wheeled the van about and drove casually back past the house, turning east at the stop sign, once again back on the highway.

Clara and Amy were lying on their sides facing one another. There was no hope, only fear in each ones eyes. Both of them were beyond crying. Clara started reciting the Lords prayer. Amy joined her. Snap heard this and laughed. Fum turned on the radio. He laughed too. Oh yeah, they both laughed, in relief, and, in anticipation. They were tuned in to the same channel and they were going to have FUN after all the risk they had taken for these two broads. Lots of fun, for a long, long time.

John Lacey and Anthony Lazaro were giggling like kids that had just pulled some stupid prank and knew that they weren't going to be caught. At this point, they were both quite insane. Still, Fum remained a very dangerous man, plus, his adopted little brother would do anything he said. Fum couldn't be sure, but he thought that Snap would probably die for him. Fum liked the little monster, but he wouldn't die for anyone, and he wasn't going to make it easy to get himself killed either.

. . .

Agents Richardson and Bottoms got the phone call from Frank Kohler before they got to the little general store where Sally Granger was last seen. She and her brothers were still a mystery as to their whereabouts. It would remain that way for a while yet. They turned around and sped towards Freeport. Sam was on the radio ordering a helicopter to rendezvous with them so they could get on the trail of the giant while it was hot.

. . .

Currently, Sally Granger was feeding the fire ants, who had driven off the swarming flies. The damn yellow jackets wouldn't leave. No matter, there was plenty to eat. Crayfish were starting to nibble on her brothers who had wound up in the summertime-shallow creek. The blood had attracted the little critters. Some vile looking water snakes had also been attracted by the blood and were now gobbling up the crayfish. An opossum was watching all this, waiting for her turn on the mountain of meat that Bubba and Duke had become, wondering dully if the snakes were the kind that would eat her babies. They were clinging to her back, too young to leave their Momma, but old enough to travel outside her pouch. They were afraid of the violent, thick bodied snakes and wished that their Momma would take them away. A huge cottonmouth snake had been trailing the possum with his tongue, running the scent through his very effective Jacobsen's organ, a tool every bit as sensitive as a hound dog's nose. Being a pit viper, he could also see the heat shimmers from the 'possum's warm body now that he was almost upon her. Mother nature has her own dramas playing out and everyone has to eat, even the lowest forms of life.

. . .

Fum was starving and asked Snap if he was hungry. Snap said that he was always hungry.

They taped the girls mouths again and stopped at the next gas station, thinking it was time to fill-er-up and check the earl. There was a large canopy over the gas pumps for the comfort of customers who had to fill their cars on rainy days. At that moment, a helicopter with the FBI logo flew over the gas station. It was heading to Freeport at ninety miles per hour with, you guessed it, Sam and Jim, the agents and long time friends who had so much respect for each other's capabilities. Twenty minutes later, they flew over a white, unmarked squad on silent alarm. They didn't pay much attention to the speeding vehicle. They were looking for a gray van with tinted windows and Texas license plate FEFIFO7.

Snap, forgetting his disguise, hopped out without his shirt and hat, wearing the sunglasses that he'd grown to like along with what most people would call a "shit eating grin". Fum had to take a leak, real bad. He untucked his tent sized shirt and stuck the .44 in his waistband, just in case. Lumbering towards the gas station looking for all the world like an oncoming freight train, the attendant watched in awe as Fum, who looked huge from afar, got bigger and bigger and bigger the closer he got. The attendant found himself reciting "Fe Fi Fo Fum", in his head as the giant got closer to the door. Then he looked at the shorter man with the Arnold Swarzeneggar body and thought, "Damn if that little monster don't look familiar." While he was looking at the deadly duo, Clara and Amy were looking at each other.

When the door opened, the giant ducked his head to get inside. The attendant thought, "That is a seven foot, commercial, glass door. This is one big dude!" He could hear a loud pounding. He thought maybe it was his heart, but it grew more quiet when the door closed behind the big dude. The shorter man with all the muscles spun around and ran back out towards the van. When the attendant looked back at the giant, he was staring into the muzzle of a hand held cannon.

"Put your hands where I can see them," ordered Fum in a calm, deadly voice. He was smiling. He knew that the girls in the van had started kicking the sides of the van, just like he knew that Snap had picked up on it and was attending to that very problem right now while he was going to deal with this one. When he saw the attendants empty hands appear on the counter, he shot him in the face. The face disappeared and the glass behind the middle aged fat man shattered. Again Fum laughed. He laid the revolver on the counter and walked around to the cash register. First things first. Fum pissed all over the dead attendant. Then he cleaned out the cash register.

Snap came back in and started putting food and sodas in a cooler that was on sale for three ninety nine which was suddenly marked down to 'free' at this moment in time. Fum zipped up and started loading another one of the 'free' coolers with 'free' food. He had a bad feeling that they would need some provisions for a spell. He had a pretty good idea where to go to hole-up.

"Let's go partner," said Fum. Snap didn't need to be asked twice. They ran to the van. The genius had left his gun on the counter. A fact that wouldn't sink in until it was too late. He would be grateful to those two dumb hillbilly brothers of that luscious Sally girl who was still feeding the ants. Yeah, Duke and Bubba had each bequeathed him their rifles when they passed away in such an untimely fashion.

H is gratitude would be very brief when he discovered that the bolt action antiques had only one round apiece in their chambers. The rest of the ammunition was in the glove box of their junky old pickup which was upside down in a ravine formed by a creek that had an alarming number of water snakes, who were once again feeding as voraciously as the ants.

Minutes after Snap and Fum drove away, Mrs. Johnson and her worthless husband pulled into the gas station they had just vacated. Spike Johnson told his wife that he was too drunk to walk, so his freckled wife went in to buy the jerk some cigarettes. She didn't mind going in because Leroy, the attendant always said something nice to her. He was kind of fat, but he wasn't near as ugly as Spike had become. That and the fact that he stayed sober at least five days a week had Mrs. Johnson dreaming about running away with the nice gentleman. She noticed the huge gun on the counter before she looked up at the broken glass. She put two and two together easily enough. After all, she was a teacher, wasn't she? She ran around the counter to call the police on the only phone in the store. To add insult to injury, she threw up all over the nice gentleman with no face who smelled like somebody had urinated on him.

She ran out the door waving her hands and screaming. Spike found out that he could walk after all. As a matter of fact, he found out that he could run too. He commenced to running away from his screaming wife. He knew something had scared her awful and the drunken coward wanted no part of anything that would make Mrs. Johnson scream.

The freckled teacher stopped in her tracks. Her world had been turned upside down. The husband that she used to love dearly was a drunk, and he was leaving her alone to God knows what, *and*, the man of her dreams no longer had a face, *plus* the nice gentleman smelled like pee and puke. These sobering thoughts brought her back to reality. She walked around to the side of the gas station, her shoes crunching on broken glass, and reached through the shattered window picking up the phone. After she called 911, she called her sister. "Brenda, it's me Linda. Remember how you always told me to leave Spike? Well, I'm doing it." Then Linda Johnson hung up to wait for the police.

Spike was running out of breath and staggering down the middle of the road. A white car came speeding out of nowhere swerving in the niche of time before putting Spike out of his misery. Linda was watching and said, "Shit!" It was the first time in her life, but it seemed appropriate to the freckle-faced teacher. Then she took out her compact and prettied herself up for the police who would be arriving soon. Leroy was gone, and she was moving on.

Sam Bottoms had guaranteed Detective Kohler that John Lacey would head back east. In his haste to be doing something, anything, Frank believed him. He didn't know that Agent Bottoms held all cops in contempt and wanted the Freeport detective out of the way. He thought he could rationalize his deception by saying that Kohler's judgment might be clouded and he couldn't have a cop with a 'shoot on sight' agenda going after the man who had kidnapped his wife. He even radioed some bogus information to Frank confirming that the van was spotted on the east-bound county road.

. . .

I was buckled in with the rifle across my knees, watching the white line appear as spots. I thanked the Lord silently that Frank was a good driver. He seemed calm and we were eating up the miles. We passed a gas station and almost hit some drunk running down the middle of the road.

There was a bad moment when we swerved, but Frank got control of the car. The radio crackled out the news of the gas station robbery. We looked at each other and Frank slowed enough to turn around. It had to be connected. The drunk was now on the shoulder, walking towards the gas station. We were the first to respond. There was a woman waiting outside who seemed remarkably calm herself. She seemed like a woman who was very much in charge of her life and capable of dealing with any emergency.

"No, I didn't see anyone. There were no other vehicles when I pulled in with that damn drunk out there in the road. He used to be my husband," said the lady.

I glanced quickly at her left hand to see a white spot on her ring finger where she'd obviously worn a band for quite some time. If I read the situation right, I figured that the ring had been tossed in her purse moments ago, but years long overdue. She had been heading east and had seen no van. That meant that the van was still heading east. We left her to wait alone for the county police, resuming our mad dash in that direction, certain that we'd catch up to our prey any minute. We had wasted a few precious minutes at the gas station, but the .44 on the counter confirmed that Agent Bottoms had given us good information.

It was almost dark now. Frank slowed down to a safer speed. The tail lights in the distance suddenly went out. I told Frank that a dark colored vehicle that looked like a van had just turned into the trees. He said, "I thought the car had gone over the hill, but you could be right, this road is pretty flat as far as I can see. Look, those headlights in the distance are level with ours."

. . .

Fum's sharp eyes found what he was looking for. He had found the winding car path where they had killed Sally Two and her brothers. Snap recognized it at the same time and figured it was show time for the ladies. They hadn't driven more than a minute or so when Snap thought that Fum was being too quiet and he was suddenly afraid of the big man. Fum was concentrating on driving between the trees in the twilight made even darker by all the branches. "I'm gonna go back and check on the girls," Snap told the big man.

Fum's mind was capable of entertaining two thoughts at once and his other thought was that his little buddy sounded strange when he said that. He stopped the van and turned around in his seat. Snap was already pointing one of the rifles at him. The little monster was actually pulling on the trigger, but he had left the safety on. Snap had said that he knew nothing about guns and he just proved that and one other thing to the big man. Fum had overestimated his partner's loyalty. Little Tony jammed the rifle at the giants face like a sword. Now it was Fum's turn to snap, and it was horrible. He got caught hard in the forehead by the muzzle of the rifle and lost control of his anger for the first time, ever. His attack wasn't an orderly assault. His size worked against him as he scrambled over the console into the back. The girls were being crushed and battered by his bulk as he tried to grab Snap who had somehow figured out how to open the doors from within. Fum thought he had them rigged against just that very thing. The little monster had spent enough time back there to figure it out. "What the hell else had the little shit been up to," thought the giant as he wriggled clumsily over Clara and Amy and crawled out the back door after the object of his sudden rage. He stopped in his tracks as he heard the unmistakable sound of a car slowing down rapidly. It could only mean one thing.

**F**um grabbed Amy by her legs and jerked her out the back door, knowing that it would slow down the pursuit. He was still hoping to keep the bigger woman for later. The giant was back to thinking again. He was the dangerous killer once more and not some enraged beast. He got back behind the wheel and drove to the ravine. Stopping at the edge, he cut the engine and retrieved both rifles. He was already painfully aware that the .44 had been left at the gas station on the counter. Only now did he discover that both deer rifles were single shot with only one round in each chamber. He was so rattled that he never thought to climb down to search the old pickup for more bullets. No matter, he had surprise on his side. He'd just ambush the cop and the big half-breed the same way he killed Duke and Bubba. Those jerks had been too easy. He rightfully assumed that his pursuers were the men he last saw with the two broads. He took both rifles off safety and picked out a big tree to lay his ambush.

Fum was partially right thinking that Amy would slow down the pursuit when she was found. Naturally Frank stopped the car and checked on his wife and Cottonmouth didn't fault him one bit for that action. Cottonmouth figured that he could run faster than a vehicle could wend it's way through the woods in the dark and he was right.

Sprinting like a deer, Walking Bear's only son flew through the pines in a straight line, something else the van couldn't do. He followed the sound of the engine.

I heard the van stop close ahead and slowed my headlong dash to a quiet walk. My father had taught me to stalk deer as a small boy and I'd done that very thing often. I heard one of the doors open on the van. One of the bad guys must have remained inside. My imagination painted some horrible pictures about what the other man was doing to Clara. I couldn't help her if I was dead so I remained cautious. Dropping to my hands and knees, I crawled closer. There was a man standing there with a rifle in each hand. It looked like he was taking them both off safe. The guy was a half of a foot taller than me and looked to be seventy or eighty pounds heavier. Again I'd left the rifle in the squad. There was no time to go back. I'd have to face this armed giant without it. The big man looked around and hurried to a tree not ten feet in front of me, leaning one rifle and pointing the other at the van. It looked like he was going to ambush his partner when he came out.

Frank was peeling the duct tape off Amy when about two hundred and five pounds of animal called Snap jumped on his back. He figured to make swift work of the middle aged cop even if he was pretty big. Snap found himself fighting for his life in a heartbeat.

Frank was no slouch in a street fight and had never lost to a thug before. Now he fighting for Amy's life as well as his own and he had to win. He bunched up his neck muscles to keep from being choked to death by the iron like hold around his neck. He had to squeeze his eyes tightly shut as Snap started raking his face from behind, trying to tear out Frank's eyes. He couldn't escape the superhuman grip of the youngster. Frank got to his feet with Snap's legs wound around his waist and still caught in that suffocating head lock. It was obvious that his attacker had training as a wrestler. The cop deliberately fell backward, hard. That did the trick. Snap had hit his head on a tree root and was out cold.

rank opened his eyes, gasping for breath. Amy had gotten the riot gun out of the squad and was pointing it at Snap. Frank said, "Don't do it Amy."

"Put the cuffs on him and I won't," she said. "If he won, I'd have killed him and liked it. Now I want to see him in the electric chair or hang or gag in the gas chamber or all of them at once. He deserves to suffer." Then she started shaking and sat down. Frank cuffed Snap's left hand to his right ankle and trundled him into the caged part of the squad.

Fum sensed too late that someone was behind him. Before he could turn, Cottonmouth had gotten to his feet and charged the giant. Fum thought that Snap was the fastest human alive. He was about to meet someone faster and much bigger.

The big man tensed as I was flying through the air with both feet aimed at the middle of his back. I struck before he could turn and he slammed into the tree, dropping the rifle. He bounced back, falling on top of me. I was still at his back, even if he was on top. I wrapped my arms and legs around him and rolled us both several feet from the rifles. Suddenly the ground disappeared. We were tumbling down an embankment. I had to let go to keep from getting my brains dashed out. We rolled over the body of a woman. When we finally stopped rolling, I found out that I had fire ants all over me. I regained my feet before the bigger man did and jumped on him again, ignoring the stings of the ants. For an instant, it looked like he was smiling. Then his face took on the appearance of a demon. It was contorted in rage and at that moment, was the ugliest thing I'd ever seen. The big man frightened me like no one ever had before in my life. Then I thought of Clara and my fear vanished. I renewed my frenzied assault, thinking to kill this demon giant as quickly as possible. I broke free and got to my feet. When he tried to get up, I kicked him under the chin. He fell down into the shallow water. I saw the snake before he landed on it. Even in the dark, I could tell that it was a cottonmouth. They were the only dark colored snakes around here that had such a big head. It had been a monster of a snake as thick as one of my arms.

Fum hurt everywhere, but the burning pain radiating from the snake-bite was like nothing in this world. He was already exhausted from the stress and the adrenaline of the fight with the half breed. Any other time, he might have survived the snake's bite. This time he was gripped by a massive heart attack. The 'possum had gotten away from the snake. The Cottonmouth had been feeding on the fat water snakes, not wasting any venom on the easier prey. Fum had gotten a full dose of poison.

Agkistrodon Piscivoros, the snake's Latin name, translates into 'fish eater', which is a misnomer. A cottonmouth will eat anything it can fit into its huge mouth, including other snakes.

I could tell that the giant was near death since his violent thrashing had changed to shallow, labored breathing. His eyes were starting to close. This wasn't an act. I couldn't see where the snake was, hopefully still under the dying man. I was wasting time down here with Clara up on top going through God only knew what kinds of horror.

I clambered up the hill, avoiding the woman's body. I was disoriented and it took a second to find the van. The banging started so suddenly that it startled me. I recovered one of the rifles and opened the rear doors. Clara was in there alone, bound with duct tape as Amy had been. Headlights were approaching. The other man still wasn't accounted for and I thought it best to hide until the car got here. I put a finger to my lips and Clara nodded at me, closing her eyes. I hoped that she was praying for us.

When Frank and Amy got out of the squad, it was like a family reunion. I could see the other man in the back seat, effectively hog-tied with cuffs, very ingenious. I turned my attention back to Clara and started by kissing her over the tape. I unbound her hands first and she threw her arms around my neck with a strength rivaling that of the giant. Amy helped with the rest of the tape, sympathetic for her friend's ordeal. I could hear siren's approaching. Help was on its way. Frank had wisely called for backup.

. . .

Cottonmouth and Clara were married in a church one year to the day after the bank robbery that bound them together for life.

Detective Frank Kohler was right, Cottonmouth turned out to be a very good cop, and detective.

Today, Cottonmouth is raising his two sons, Walker B. and Franklin X. Crown to be policemen too. Snap is still on death row. He is no longer a young man, and his nightmares have pushed him over the edge. He is a broken man who will eventually run out of appeals and be executed. On that day, Amy Kohler will decide not to attend, and hold a picnic instead.

When Fum's body was winched by cable to the top of the ravine, Cottonmouth watched a very healthy, and very poisonous, five-foot long Western Cottonmouth slither into the water. He thought about killing the beast, but let it go. It occurred to him that the Lord might have sent that snake to him just like he, Cottonmouth, had been sent to Clara.

# MIKE'S PLACE

The Lonesome River earned its name, for the land that it meandered through. It was so desolate that the true course of the river is incorrect on most maps. Corrections on the newer maps were made from satellite photography. In my part of Florida, the river was sixty feet wide in summer and up to a half mile wide when it flooded. Alligators and alligator gar were the most common animals in the river. Cottonmouths and Eastern Diamondbacks were the prevalent snakes on the banks of this inhospitable body of water. Throw in most of the larger species of water snakes and it was downright inhospitable.

I lived about three miles away on a piece of high ground in a town so little that its name was Smallville. A gas station and a grocery store took up most of Main Street on the East Side. There was a tiny post office and a Baptist Church on the West Side. There were a few houses mixed in for people who liked city life, plus a bar and grill to round out our metropolis. The rest of the population was hidden throughout the woods in trailers. Mobile homes to some, but the bottom line is that they came in on wheels.

The handful of kids in town were bussed seven miles away to school in a town just big enough to have a school. It was a small town but people hadn't taken to looking like each other if you get my drift. Most folks worked in the city about fifty miles off. The drive was necessary to keep from starving to death. Speaking of death, the tiny cemetery by the church didn't get much action.

This part of the state was warm all winter and unbearably hot in summer. We were at one of those in between times when the weather was just beautiful. Today, Saturday, I took a ride out to the bridge on one of the countless curves of the river. Like the river, I was lonesome and was used to doing things alone. As a matter of fact, I truly liked being alone. I knew that someday, some sweet talking girl would confuse me enough to get me to the altar. Until that day I would just go on being alone and quietly happy.

I was leaning on the guard rail and reflecting on my recent past. The war in Vietnam had just ended. Four years ago, I had played a role in that action that I would always be proud of. I had been infantry which was as involved as one could get. It meant a real close-up look at the monster simply called war. I wasn't very big when I was there. As a matter of fact, I was only 5'6" and 130 pounds back then. I walked point so the weight just melted off my stressed out self. Since I got out of the army, I had done nothing but lift weights when I wasn't at work, and eat like a horse. Even my job as a shingle installer on roofs built muscle. I had packed on forty-five solid pounds in the last four years or so. My black hair and dark tan came from the Cherokee on my Dad's side of the family.

The alligators were astir over something big just a few yards downstream. It was already dead but I was curious because it looked sort of human. I picked up some chunks of concrete under the bridge and spotted a nearby heavy piece of driftwood. Holding the chunks to my chest, I picked up the driftwood and went to see what I could see.

I started bouncing the concrete off the alligators and beating the water with the driftwood. It was no small task to get them to give up their meal. It was pretty obvious that it used to be human. It was either a man with long hair or a woman.

Still pounding the water with the wood, I grabbed one of its hands and dragged it well up the bank. I walked back to my pickup and used my cell phone to call the County Sheriff. I told him that I'd guard the body from 'gators until he arrived. If I hadn't gotten there when I did, the body would have been totally unrecognizable. It must have been recently dumped to look as fresh as it did.

The Sheriff and the Coroner both showed up. They made their way down to me. I told them why I had to disturb the body. The Coroner said, "You were crazy for doing it but you did the right thing. At least now I have something to examine."

"Lord, I hope she was dead before she hit the water," I said. Both men nodded their agreement.

The Coroner went back to his ambulance and got a board with some straps. I helped him carry Jane Doe up the sloping riverbank. He noted the time as the Sheriff looked around for any clues. They got my phone number and address and thanked me again. I supposed that I'd have to read about it in the paper. The body looked fresh and that bothered me. It was almost certainly thrown in the river this morning, maybe within the hour.

I figured that the Sheriff had only wanted my name and address because I was a suspect. Instead, I got a call from him. He asked if he could see me.

"At the river or at my house?" I inquired. He said that he'd rather come to my house. So I left the once peaceful river and headed to my empty trailer. He was there within the hour. I let him in and started the coffee pot.

The conversation at first was about the dead woman. She was a teacher from the school seven miles away. Her children had called the police when she hadn't returned from a quick trip to the store in over two hours. Her car had been found in the parking lot and an all points bulletin had been put out on her. The children were with an aunt trying to adjust to the awful news.

"Now here's where you come in," said the Sheriff. "We need someone to watch that bridge twenty- four hours per day. I'd like to deputize you and let you be our watch-dog. We will provide you with an M-16 rifle and a .38 special revolver. Also, we'll give you a camouflage tent and a case of C-rations. I had you checked out. I'm already aware of your military background. I'll square it with your boss to be off work. We can only pay patrolman's wage. You'll receive a police radio and assigned the call sign 'Gate Keeper.' If you have any further needs, express them now."

"I'll need an entrenching tool, a camping shovel won't do. I also want a machete and a fine file to sharpen both items. I'll have to have water purification tablets too. The tent can't be shiny. It must have a dull finish. I also need to know the pertinent call signs on your side of the operation," I said.

Now the Sheriff spoke up, "The prowl car nearest you will be "Golden Gate", I'll be "Base" and I can cover all your requests within the hour. I'll have an unmarked car drop you and wait until you're set up."

"One more thing, if it's possible, I'd like a dog. He'll be priceless on helping me pull guard." The dog was granted instantly as a very good idea. The Sheriff never said that he thought there was a serial killer but the plans that he was making indicated that he did.

The Sheriff was good for his word. Within the hour, my gear was delivered along with two sets of camouflage fatigues that I hadn't thought to ask for.

I was outside making friends with the big German Shepherd named Trouble when Sheriff Jim Goodson showed up. He was in an unmarked car so I surmised that he would drop me off and watch my setup. I threw my gear in his trunk and got in the back seat to do some bonding with Trouble.

On the trip out to the bridge, the Sheriff made a confession. The teacher was not the first body. Herpetologists had found another female's remains not far downstream from where I'd spotted the teacher. That one hadn't been identified yet. He was pretty sure that the remains would turn out to be those of another missing woman from Granger, where the teacher was kidnapped. He was also pretty sure that there would be others and he hoped that our little ambush would end all this.

"Shoot the tires first, defend yourself if you have to, and call 'Golden Gate' ASAP. Golden gate will call me enroute. And no more pulling up the bodies alone, wait for help. Now raise your right hand and repeat after me. "I, Alfred Benson, do swear to uphold the laws of the county, to serve and protect the citizens therein." That was the longest conversation that Goodson and I had for quite a while. I had a feeling that this might be an interesting assignment.

He dropped me at the bridge and had me point out where I would set up and tell him why. I said that I would set up under the bridge since I would be completely out of sight and the killer or killers were almost certainly dumping the bodies over the bridge. He said that he approved of my plan and drove away.

So there we were, Trouble and me, on a lark at the river. That dog looked like trouble too. In a fair fight with no weapons, most men would go down. First I moved our gear under the bridge. Then I started poking around with the machete. A big, fat Cottonmouth crawled out to meet my challenge. Naturally I chopped off its head. I flung the still writhing body into the river where it was immediately snatched by some lucky gar. I speared the dangerous head and whipped it into the river. Whatever ate that probably wouldn't live. I poked around some more and stirred up another, bigger cottonmouth which went the way of the first one.

Now I could make a shelter. I centered it under the bridge and wished for a dozen king snakes to help with my venomous neighbors. Maybe the Sheriff could requisition some Indigo Snakes instead from a local pet store. I'd be sure to ask base if that was possible.

Water came from the river and only in the daytime. They gave Trouble some dried dog food that required water to make it palatable. I got my case of C-rations as requested. I also got seven full magazines for the M-16 and fifty rounds for my .38 special. Loading both, I put the .38 in my pocket and slung the M-16 across my back. Then I scraped a flat spot under the bridge big enough for Trouble and me to sleep on. Now to sharpen some stakes to make an alligator fence. A double row pushed into the ground facing outward. This would require a lot of wood, which meant machete work.

I had Trouble heel as I walked to the tree line being on the watch for snakes. This river's reputation was frightening. I made sixty stakes and carried as many as possible back to camp. This time I told Trouble to stay and left the rifle and machete hidden in the tent. Hastening back to my cache of sharpened stakes, I was able to carry the remainder back in one trip. Dark was only an hour and a half away. There was no time to rest.

I felt a lot better with the fence in place. Now we could eat and get some sleep. I made my way through the fence to get some water. I hauled it in a five- quart flexible canteen called a 'blivet'. After putting ten iodine tablets in and sloshing it around, I fed Trouble first. Then I made some coffee and heated up some C-rations. By now it was quite dark and I was ready for sleep. I believed that the killers operated in the daytime anyway.

Sleep wouldn't come for me. It was too quiet and more than a little spooky out here. To make matters worse, fog was moving in. I felt like I was in a scary movie and my murderer was creeping up on me using the veil of the fog to draw ever nearer. The dog was asleep. That was my barometer. I quit scaring myself and eventually dozed off.

The dog and I both woke up every time a car neared the bridge, but none of them stopped. I woke up at sunrise to the sound of birds. I hadn't slept outside in years. I had forgotten how loud the birds were. Trouble had slept next to me all night. Now he got up and stretched and yawned. Then he gave me that, "What's for breakfast?" look. I took his bowl down to the river to wash it. First I looked for 'gators carefully. I had a lot of respect for them. They were easier to deal with when one knew where they were. So with the pistol in one hand, I washed the bowl with the other. Now Trouble looked happy as I stirred his chow together.

Having fed the livestock, I made some coffee and warmed up a meal all with only two heat tabs. Soon the traffic picked up leaving Smallville and going to Granger. This traffic was much lighter than the traffic heading towards the city of Crete. Even some of the folks of Granger had to commute to Crete. After a while the school bus went overhead. Now the traffic was very sporadic as the shoppers went on their ways. Trouble had woven his way through the alligator fence to do his business and jumped over it coming back. My turn next. I could only hope that no cars would come. I went inside the tree line and hoped that my camouflage worked. On the way out, I chopped up a rattler with the military shovel [entrenching tool]. When I got back, I'd call base and request those Indigo Snakes. They were way bigger than king snakes and had a faster metabolism, so they ate more and ate more often.

Slipping back to camp unnoticed, I wished for a book to read and a radio to keep abreast of the news. I called base and asked Sheriff Goodson for some books and a radio. Then I told him about my snake problem. He said that by noon, he'd come out with my needs. That would work out fine since the killer or killers seemed to be the morning type.

When the Sheriff showed up, the first thing that he said was that the snakes were $180.00 apiece. I knew that ahead of time but was afraid to tell him. They were five feet long with the capacity to reach seven to nine feet in a few years. They were three times the diameter of a five foot king snake. I was happy anyway.

The books were westerns, probably from the Sheriff's personal collection. The small transistor radio came with several extra batteries. He had even brought out a jug of all purpose liquid soap. I thanked him profusely. Now I was in good shape. It broke his heart to watch me put $360.00 worth of snakes on the ground only to see them crawl swiftly away. One went to the cubby hole under the bridge. I could hear him thrashing about as if he had already found something to eat.

He was impressed with the alligator fence. "I was wondering how you were going to deal with that problem," he said. "You have all the ingenuity I gave you credit for." He said that he had to leave so the operation wasn't compromised.

So there we were, just the three of us, Trouble and me and boredom. I could read a book. Trouble had nothing to amuse himself with so I took him for a walk in the trees on the other side of the bridge. They came much closer here on the high bank. A few cars went by but no one stopped. The dog had found a tortoise and he seemed perplexed that the head and feet disappeared. All that I had to do was say "No" and Trouble left the tortoise alone.

The rest of the day passed uneventfully. I read an entire novel, out loud at first, but the dog fell asleep so I read to myself. I got my cooking done before dark. Light discipline might be a life or death issue. Tonight was a mirror of last night with us waking whenever a car approached, again, none of them stopped.

Our morning went like the previous one until about 9:30. A car stopped overhead. I crept toward the blind side of the bridge and spied on our visitor. Naturally Trouble was at my heel sniffing the air. It was a newer vehicle, four door hard top with Florida plates, which I memorized.

The dog seemed highly agitated, even hostile. I decided to risk a closer look. There was a couple in the car. The man looked much older than his female companion. They appeared to be kissing and generally enjoying each other's company. I could hear another car and the first car took off. I continued to watch from my concealed position. The new car kept going. I figured that car number one was trying to save on motel costs. They seemed to be getting along well enough.

I went back to the camp and immediately heard another vehicle approaching from the direction that car one had gone. They slowed down as they approached the bridge. This time I would have to spy from the other side of the bridge.

As expected, the car stopped. It was the four-door sedan again. This time their kissing must have gotten out of hand because she was telling him to quit it in a loud voice. When she screamed, Trouble and I made ourselves known. It was already too late to save the girl. Her neck seemed broken. The man put his car in gear and tried to run me over. Trouble jumped into the passenger window and commenced to make the driver wish he were somewhere else. I commanded the dog to hold and he quit mutilating our aging Don Juan.

I approached the driver's door and waved the man out with the M-16. Trouble followed him out the driver's door. "Face down and spread eagle. That dog will kill you on command." Next I scrambled under the bridge and brought up the radio. I called Golden Gate and went to search the captive. He didn't even have so much as a pocket-knife. I told the dog "Watch." The girl in the car surprised me by speaking.

"My neck hurts," she said. "He choked me," she said pointing at the man under Trouble's intimidating watch. She stepped out of the car and came to stand by me.

I told her that a squad was coming. I also told her that her friend was a suspect in multiple murders. She got real quiet then, just staring at the man on the ground. The squad's siren could be heard as it approached. Gatekeeper pulled up shortly and cuffed my captive.

"Congratulations Alfred, let's hope that this is our man and not just a coincidence," said the deputy. Base pulled up next followed by a tow truck. The car had to get a thorough going over by the crime scene investigators. If they couldn't tie some evidence from the car to the most recent victim, it could easily be a coincidence. The girl got in with Goodson who told me to stay put and await further instructions. Everybody was out of there in twenty minutes. Luckily no other cars had gone by, so my position wasn't compromised. This time I put on the local news to see if the Sheriff was leaking any tidbits to the media. After an hour of listening, I was convinced that our Sheriff was too smart to put anything in the news.

Trouble and I spent another night waking as every car went by. The morning went the same way, listening to traffic and the rumble of the school bus. Everything was routine until almost 10:30 AM when a car stopped on the bridge. I crept to my spy position with the dog at my side. The dog was agitated again.

What I saw this time was dismal. The driver, a white male in his early thirties was driving a black pickup with a snap top cover over the bed. He undid a few snaps and lowered the tailgate. Next he reached into the bed and grabbed a dead women by the hair and dragged her out, letting her drop on the ground. I let Trouble initiate the attack as I got into a position to make escape impossible. I called the dog off and told the man to stay on the ground.

I told him to look up so he could see that I was armed. Then I put my knee in his back and frisked him. He was carrying a five shot, .32 caliber revolver, which I stuck in one of the big pockets of my fatigue pants. I told Trouble to watch him and reminded the man that if he moves, the dog will kill him. I went for the radio and called Golden Gate to tell him that the drill would be repeated except that we'd need an ambulance and the Coroner. I scrambled back topside to help trouble watch our tough killer of women.

Soon the bridge was full of vehicles. Goodson was patting me on the back and Trouble picked up on his mood so he came over to be petted. The Coroner patched up the suspect's bites and Golden Gate put the jerk in the back of his squad. The tow truck took the pickup. I helped the Coroner with the body again. The Sheriff told me this time to pack up my gear and he'd give me a ride home. He walked away muttering about $360.00 worth of snakes. Me, I had a feeling that I'd be out behind my alligator fence again someday soon. I just hope those Indigo Snakes stuck around.

It really would feel good to be home again. I wasn't sure that I wanted to go back to roofing, but I had to eat and that was the best way I knew how to make a living. After Goodson dropped me at my house, my first stop was the shower. I decided to take the rest of the day off.

Sheriff Goodson called after a while and asked how I liked police work. I told him that I enjoyed working alone, but would it pay my bills? He told me the yearly starting salary and described the benefits. It matched my yearly average and I didn't even have benefits. "Keep talking, Sheriff, it's sounding better all the time." That was the birth of my new career. Now I was glad that I was home to receive the call. I told him that I liked special assignments like the one I had just completed.

He told me to keep the camouflage handy and asked if I could come by the station today. We set an appointment. I wondered if I could put up with the regimental life of a deputy. Then I remembered the benefits and retirement program. I guess that all made it worth it. At any rate, I wasn't going to be late for the appointment with the Sheriff. Besides, I still had the jerk's pistol in my pocket.

I dressed in jeans and a T-shirt and drove to Granger to see the chief. I couldn't help but stop on the bridge and look over both sides. I was only minimally surprised to see a body in the water. I got on the cell phone and called Sheriff Goodson. He seemed to be shocked to silence. I told him that I would wait on the bridge. Fifteen minutes later he showed up followed shortly by another squad. I told him that we would need a boat to get this one unless he wanted to swim out there. We waited for a boat to show up as we watched the gar destroying evidence. I surrendered the .32 revolver and explained the oversight.

Thirty-five minutes later, a boat approached swiftly from the direction of Granger. The Coroner showed up while they were dragging the corpse into the boat. I went down to the water to help out. The Coroner climbed down with his board and straps. Another woman, probably killed this morning. Two bodies in one day. Who'd have guessed? Suddenly I felt very tired. These bodies used to be nice people. What kind of gaping holes were they leaving in which families? Who was grieving? It looked as if I was joining the force when they really needed help as well as moral support. It was all so overwhelming. Nothing was simple about this case or cases. This mystery was going to require a lot of footwork plus my stakeout back here at the bridge. A man feels really helpless at a time like this. There were as many possibilities as stars in the night sky. I hope that the Sheriff had already given this problem some thought. He said that the body I found wasn't the first.

The boat went back as quickly as it had come. The Coroner's ambulance left along with the other squad. Jim Goodson and I lingered long enough for him to ask me if I'd man the bridge again.

"Sure," I said, trying to sound enthusiastic. But I'm sure that I looked as drained as he did. He followed me to my house so I could pick up my gear and drop off my truck. I asked for Trouble again plus two cases of fresh water. That river water was gross tasting, especially with the iodine in it. Jim shook my hand and thanked me for doing a dirty and frightening job.

"Just get Trouble out here so I can be brave," I told him.

By the time the Sheriff arrived, I had the tent back up and was drinking coffee. Trouble was glad to see me. I lugged the water down to the tent and went back up to shoot the breeze with Jim. I suggested that they give serious thought to dragging the river from here downstream a quarter mile. "There are almost certainly more remains on the bottom. That's not what I want, that's what I suspect."

The Sheriff had to agree with me. He looked older than when I first met him a few days ago.

"My department doesn't have that kind of equipment. We'll have to involve either the State Patrol or the FBI," was his tired reply.

I suggested that we carry on as we had been for another week. "There may be more fish to fry that would only be scared away with the kind of disturbance a dragging operation would create." He gave in to my suggestion for the same reason. That was our cue to say goodbye.

So there we were again, a man and his dog, but what a dog. I felt safe at night with his natural radar working. Not to mention that he'd die for me, and he didn't look like he would die easily. Trouble was smart too. He knew enough to jump the alligator fence and he wasn't running around in the open chasing rabbits. That first night back, the fog returned as spooky as the last time.

Around 12:30 AM a car stopped on the bridge. Trouble and I crept to our usual spot for a car coming from Granger. We had to creep closer because of the fog.

There were two middle aged white males in an El Camino taking a parcel out of the back. It was rolled in a bloody carpet and it looked like a person. I raised my M-16 and crept closer. "Freeze" I shouted.

They didn't seem overly surprised which made me very suspicious. I made them lie down spread eagle. Then I called the dog and told him to "Watch."

As I was searching the two on the ground, I heard a noise in the back of their vehicle. Turning, I saw a man sitting up with a machine pistol pointing at me. I blew the smile off his face with a short burst on automatic from the rifle and swung my attention back to the jokers on the ground. Trouble was growling like one of them had moved. I continued my search of the suspects and found four guns and two knives. I made the two men come under the bridge with me so I could call Golden Gate and base. We had about five minutes to get to know each other before the first prowl car showed up. I already had the suspects standing on the bridge with their hands clasped on their heads. The patrolman cuffed them to each other and had them lie back down spread eagle. I showed him the body in the El Camino and told him that this one was rolled in a bloody carpet and I thought he was dead at first. He was shaking his head in disbelief when I told him about the ambush they'd planned.

Jim showed up about five minutes later. He was just as amazed as the patrolman had been after he heard the whole story. Then the Coroner showed up along with a tow truck. The story was repeated to the astonishment of Steve the Coroner.

I said, "This was a deliberate and nearly successful ambush. That first prisoner must have made a call to warn the rest of the operation. I think that tomorrow would be a good time to start the dredging," then I suggested that I finish the night just in case.

The Sheriff told the prowl car to set up at the stop sign by Main Street so I could have back up nearby and people would just think that he was radar. Then he told me that he would come for me after breakfast. I thanked him and everyone went their merry ways except Trouble and me. The rest of the night passed quietly, thank God.

Jim showed up just after nine. I already had my gear packed and up on the bridge. The dredging crew had already arrived. They were setting up as Jim and I drove away. The FBI was going to assist us while the State covered the dredging operation. He told me to take the day off and ring him tomorrow. I decided to shower and drive back to the dredging site expecting to find the Sheriff there.

Half an hour later I was by the bridge. It took a minute to spot Jim among the crowd. There were no civilians. My badge got me over to Goodson.

The first thing he said was that he was expecting me. Then he said, "They have already found some human bone fragments. The 'gators don't leave much."

"Where's the Coroner?" I asked.

Steve is down on one of the boats separating the animal bones from the real thing. I don't think that our first suspect is related to the mass murders. The three in the El Camino were sent specifically to kill you. That was obvious even if they weren't talking, which they weren't. Their boss must be scarier than prison. I expect to find a link between the joker in the pick-up and the three in the El Camino."

Just then, Steve the Coroner shouted to us that he found some more. We watched as he rinsed the mud off several bones and a skull.

A small clean hole could be seen in the front of the skull. I could imagine what the back looked like. I wondered if it came from a .32 caliber.

A car was approaching from Granger, when its driver saw the squads, he turned around and went back. I told Jim, "There goes some answers."

We jumped in his unmarked vehicle and sped off in hot pursuit. We caught up quickly and eventually forced the car off the road. The shooting started before we got out of the car. Luckily I had my .38 in my pocket. We scrambled out of the squad and set up a cross-fire. Goodson yelled to them to throw down their guns. They just threw more lead. Oh well, we tried.

I had the best protection by the engine with no gas tank to explode so I drew their fire up front. That enabled Jim to get a clear shot from the rear. The driver screamed and slumped over. The passenger slipped out and ran into the woods. He was a big dude, but he ran like a deer. I told Jim that I'd go after him so we wouldn't shoot one another by accident. I wished for my camouflage outfit. The jeans would make an easy target to spot. There were no trails and I could hear him crashing away to my left. I moved over to the trail that he was creating. That should make my going easier. I was gaining on him and I had to worry about him hearing me. He seemed to be going slower so I tried my best to be quiet. When I couldn't hear him any more, I started walking more carefully.

It occurred to me that he was waiting somewhere close ahead. I left his trail and made my way as quietly as possible so I wouldn't get ambushed. He had been wearing gray slacks and a black shirt. I had a slight advantage over him. I'd hunted people before.

When I got to where the insect noise had stopped, I knew that I was danger close. I was on my hands and knees now practically holding my breath. I was sure that he was in the next clearing. I would be coming out behind him. Peering through the palmettos, I saw him watching the back trail with his gun at the ready. The next move on my part would determine if I walked him back or if I would have to carry him. I drew a bead on his head and said, "Drop it!"

Like any intelligent man, he dropped it. Thank God I wouldn't have to carry his 225 lb. body. I spread-eagled him and searched him. All he had on him was a knife and that one gun. He was too dumb to carry extra clips. I told him to get on his feet and retrace his steps. A couple of times I had to point the way. He was helpless in the woods.

I hollered "Don't shoot" before we entered the roadway. Jim was out there with the car's trunk open. He was talking with a rather frightened woman.

We put the captive in the back of the squad. The body of the other man was buckled into the front seat, passenger side of his car. The woman was found tied up in the trunk. God only knows what they had planned for her. The Sheriff drove towards Granger with me following in the bad guy's car.

That was the privilege of rank. Jim has the woman in the front of his car. I ride with a stiff for a passenger. Oh well, maybe some day I would be Sheriff.

This would be my first trip to the station. I was looking forward to it. The building was much smaller than I imagined it to be. Granger was the county seat and there were only 7,000 or so people in town. Crete was in another county. I left my silent companion for the more lively company of Jim and the woman. We went up the steps and inside. It looked better than the tent I shared with Trouble.

The Sheriff turned the woman over to a lady cop. It was then that I asked what we should do about the cold one in my car.

He said, "First we'll bring in the live one and lock him up. Then two of the Coroner's white coats will come with a stretcher for the guy who can't talk. They'll take him around back and into our rather crowded morgue. Then you and I grab a cup of coffee and play detective for a while. I'll get the crime scene investigators to share some of their knowledge and send them down to the bloody car to look for more answers. There's no sense doing anything further until we've consulted with the evidence crew."

With that thought in mind, he got some coffee for us and we sat quietly in his office. A lot of paperwork goes along with shooting anyone. This made one apiece for us today and we had to get that behind us. I went and filled the cups again while Jim phoned the evidence people.

We talked while we waited. I suggested that white slavery was at work here. That's why there are so many bad guys. Someone is taking orders for and delivering women to all who could afford them. Once the captive is paid for, supply could care less what becomes of them.

Jim reminded me that everyone was afraid of supply. No one was talking. Even offers of clemency or immunity were ignored.

I said that it was as easy as showing a man a video of a live person being torn up by alligators and telling him that it would happen to him if he talks. A little audio along with the video would go a long way to convincing them just how golden silence could be. I also made the point that no one man could carry this out alone. It would take a network of bogeymen to make it work.

The Sheriff said that he had similar thoughts and was trying not to think about it. "This is the first serious crime wave that the county has ever known. These people are monsters whose only regard for human life is personal entertainment and profit. We both know that Steve will be pulling remains out of that sludge until this time next year. We have to stop these monsters even if it costs us our lives. When all of our guys report, we'll formulate a plan, no matter how dangerous, that will result in ending this nightmare. Failure is an option we can't afford."

Jim was starting to sound suicidal. The only person[s] that I wanted in danger were the perpetrators. So I said, "Jim, if you outfit me as I request, I'll infiltrate this group. All that you've got to do is keep our prisoners from communicating with the outside world. Stick them in solitary and to hell with their civil rights!"

The Sheriff was silent for a while, then he spoke slowly, "The people in this county are like my family. Why do you think that you're the best qualified and what makes you so sure that you'll be successful?"

"Jim, I just tracked, flanked and captured a man in a strange patch of woods. That wasn't luck, and it was easy for me. The other night I killed one man and captured two others. The police and the military are a lot alike. Trust me when I say that my year in Vietnam as a Pointman in the Infantry qualifies me uniquely for this task. When I start off on this little adventure, don't worry about me. Worry about the bad guys who will be lucky if they live through this." I think my last speech convinced him.

As I hoped, the crime scene investigators had many puzzle pieces to donate. Now, to interrogate the prisoners myself. Starting with the joker with the snap-top pickup and working through the survivors of the El Camino, and on to this morning's capture in the woods.

. . .

The joker confirmed my suspicions. Nothing could convince him to talk, not even placing him in witness protection. The El Camino brothers were equally silent, even though their other friend got a face full of bullets. This morning's captive would only say that the brains played too rough for him to talk. That's all that he said and he ignored all my other questions. The expression is "He wouldn't say "shit" if he had a mouthful."

Was I on square one? Almost, but once I found out who was the roughest player on the street, I was pretty much on track. People like that usually run a diversified business to include drugs and gun running and they positively won't tolerate competition. That should really narrow the field. Nobody knew my face in Granger. No one knew my name either. My biggest fear was that the police force had been infiltrated. That would be my death sentence. So after my fruitless interviews with the scum of the earth, I had to go looking for the devil. Thank God it was a small town and hopefully the devil would be easy to find.

Jim and I spoke in his office for about an hour. The first thing he said was that the body count of innocents at the bridge was still mounting. Then we commenced to discuss strategy on my introduction into Granger's society. I didn't want to die, especially on the first day. The gist of our conversation was that I would shave my head and get an apartment or rent a small house in town, preferably the house. Also I had to take my time looking for the top or bottom depending upon your personal feelings. If I was too pushy, I would be suspect. The Sheriff had another squad take me [in the back seat] to my truck back by the bridge.

I went home and started packing. I was going to miss my little trailer in the country. I left most of my things. I would keep up the payments there while the county or FBI or whoever covered the rent on my temporary home. I phoned Jim at the station to meet me in the middle somewhere so I could draw some cash. He said that an account had already been set up for me at the only bank in town which had no drive through, but which did have an ATM machine, handing me an ATM card.

When I got to the bank in Granger with my freshly shaved head, the manager approached me at the teller's window. He said that there were two accounts. One was for my policeman's pay and the other one from the FBI. That answered that question. He handed me a piece of paper with both accounts on it. Believe me, the FBI paid better. I was hoping that this man was one of the good guys. As far as I was concerned, he already knew too much just seeing my face and associating it with the FBI and police. I didn't want to wind up killing him because he was wearing a wedding band.

The next thing I did was to buy a newspaper and go to a coffee shop. Daylight was running out and I wanted to get moved in before dark. The FBI was so generous that I could afford a nice rental home. Looking through the rentals, I called the best sounding one for my needs. It was a little expensive, but available. The landlord came to the diner. The house was on the square almost straight across from the police station. It was a two story colonial. Pets were allowed. That meant that I might get Trouble for a roommate. He was sure one hell of a watchdog. The front yard was fenced in, as was the larger back yard. I would have to buy a lawnmower. Tonight I would be glad to move in before dark.

Tomorrow I would switch the utilities to my name. I would also check on Trouble. I only brought a love seat and a coffee table for living room furniture. I did remember to get my box spring and mattress, which I lugged upstairs to the master bedroom. Mercifully there were already drapes on the windows. I had my sheets and blanket rolled up like a bedroll. That was the last of my belongings.

My Lord! I was going to sleep on a bed tonight. The Goodwill store on the square would supply any more furniture needs. I decided to go to the nearest tavern just to make my quiet debut in town.

The place was surprisingly crowded. I found an empty barstool against the wall and slipped inconspicuously onto it. I could feel several pairs of eyes on me. Then I remembered my freshly shaved head. I sat there sipping my draught, looking at no one. After about my third beer, I decided that this had been enough exposure for one night. On my way out the door a gorgeous little redhead got in my way deliberately.

"Are you coming in tomorrow night?" she asked with the cutest accent I had heard in a while. I told her that I would if she was going to be there. Then I gave my most charming smile, the one that comes naturally in a situation like this. She let me pass, smiling back at me. Walking to the truck, I saw a fight in the parking lot. Just two evenly matched men, who were not even hurting each other, probably friends under normal circumstances.

I had a feeling that this was not the bad ass bar that I was looking for. It would have to do. I had to get my foot in the door and the red head already gave me that opportunity. Tomorrow would take care of itself. Tonight I was looking forward to sleeping in a bed.

I won't lie to you and say that I got to sleep right away or that I didn't think of the red headed cutie. I also worried about what kind of beasts I might turn up in a case where people were toys and life was cheap.

I checked my cell phone to see if it worked, calling the station and identifying myself as officer Benson. I asked if the Sheriff was still in. After a few minutes, Jim got on the line. He said that he was on another line with Steve. The Coroner had identified one of the remains as male. That was a puzzle. He also said that the FBI had taken the prisoners to another facility to avoid compromising my identity.

I told Jim about my short foray to the bar and my return trip tomorrow night. Then I brought up the topic of Trouble and my fenced in yard. He said that he'd meet me at the bridge tomorrow with the dog. I thanked him and said goodnight. He had my cell phone number if he needed me. "Wake me if you have to," I told my new friend.

By ten o'clock I had already been to the hardware and put eight beware of dog signs on my fence. I also padlocked the gate in the back yard. Now to go get my buddy and show him his temporary home. Driving out to the bridge, I could see how far the dredging operation had gone. Poor Steve was on one of the boats raking through the mud. He had a huge pile of bones on the barge with another set of what looked like human remains in his boat. I hailed him and he waved one muddy glove and went back to work.

The Sheriff pulled up and let the dog out. As soon as Trouble saw me, he ran up and put his paws on my shoulder. He was a bunch taller than I in this position. Looking down, he was able to look in my eyes. There was no hostility there, just friendly greetings. I transferred his weight to one arm and roughed up his fur. I had to let him down. He was just too heavy. Then he sat down on my foot like I couldn't go away.

Jim told me of a bar outside of town that might be too rough to go in alone. I said that I'd put that off until tomorrow.

He said that he was in touch with the survivor of the first incident.

From the information she disclosed, her attacker was a friend whose hormones over rode his common sense. That incident looked like that all along to me. He would do time for sexual assault but he wasn't from the bunch that we were after.

Trouble and I turned around and headed for my new home in Granger. He checked out the front yard and galloped all over the house. I let him out the back door and he ran around the bigger yard like a puppy. This beat the cages at the police pound. It really was good to have him back. I let him run loose in the yard while I went shopping for furniture and dog food. He seemed happy enough exploring the yard.

I walked the short distance to the grocery store for dog food. A fifty- pound bag should do him for a while. Shouldering my load, I went home to get my truck. The table and chairs were more than I wanted to walk with. I dropped off my load and fed and watered Trouble. Now I drove to the big supermarket at the far end of town to fill the refrigerator and get a ball and a Frisbee and a chew toy for my buddy. I was honestly looking forward to my date tonight. I hadn't been on a date for quite some time.

Driving home, I had to resist the urge to wave at a passing squad. No sense courting disaster before the operation got off the ground. I spent the remainder of the afternoon setting up furniture and playing Frisbee with the dog.

At dark I could feel the sunburn on my head starting to hurt. I showered and let the dog in. I had to get some oil or my scalp would crack and bleed. I walked across the street to the grocery store for some tanning lotion. Then I drove to the tavern where I was last night. It looked like my date was going to be fashionably late.

This time the only open seat at the bar was front center, no problem. That's how to meet people. There was a man on either side of me. I asked the lady bartender for a draught beer and started sipping it while I watched my back in the mirror over the bar. Before my glass was empty, my lady friend walked in. I spun around on my stool and our smiles came naturally. I hopped down and escorted her to a table. The barmaid came over and asked her what she needed. That told me she wasn't a regular.

I asked what her name was. "Peggy," she said. "What's yours?"

"My name is Alfred Leroy Benson, but you can call me Al." That made her laugh. She had a nice laugh, natural, not forced. Her drink showed up and I covered it plus a tip. "Do you like dogs?" I asked.

She said "Yes" and that she had a German Shepherd named Gladys. "That's perfect. I have an oversized male Shepherd named Trouble. He is my only friend in town."

"What about me?" she asked.

"You can be my friend if you want, and Gladys can be Trouble's friend."

"That sounds interesting," she said. "Could we have a few drinks before we meet each other's dogs?" she asked coyly.

"Certainly," I said. "It doesn't even have to be tonight," I said, hoping that I wasn't rushing her. That's when she told me that a friend had dropped her off so one of us would be meeting a dog. I was back on track! I waved for the barmaid to bring two more of the same.

After the second round disappeared, she said that it would probably be my dog that got the visit. She wanted to see how I lived before she showed me her home, whatever that meant. She looked nice and smelled clean so maybe it was me that she was worried about. I waved for more drinks and tipped the girl again. My intuition told me that when these drinks were empty would be a good time to show her my dog.

My intuition was right and I led her outside to my truck. She complimented my vehicle. She said that hers was in the shop. Five minutes later we were at my place. When I opened the front gate, Trouble barked once. She said that my dog sounded like a lion. Stand still when he sniffs you. When he licks your hand, it's alright to pet him. She hid behind me when I opened the door. After he greeted me, he sniffed her and licked her hand immediately. Peggy said that this dog would eat her 65 pound Gladys. I told her that Trouble liked petite women. Again she laughed that natural laugh.

I let the dog out back for a while. Peggy said that she brought her toothbrush and asked if I would like company tonight. That was the 'first' time that I kissed her.

. . .

Peggy was as much fun in the morning as she was at night. We showered together and went to breakfast. After I'd killed the bogeyman, I might move her out to Smallville with me. There was so much to find out about her before getting serious. Unfortunately I was on two payrolls to do a job that I wasn't expected to live through. The job had to come first. Thinking of the Coroner with his piles of bones made me shudder. I was the best man for this job, but even I can make mistakes.

Both of us ate like lumberjacks. I was still trying to get the taste of C-rations out of my mouth. We exchanged phone numbers and I drove her home. She had a nice house. She was living with her parents and going to the junior college just at the outskirts of town. I told her that I couldn't talk about my job yet, but I wasn't a criminal. Then I kissed her goodbye and went to work. Work for me was feeling out that rowdy bar. I know that a bar can take on quite a different personality at night. I was just looking.

I sat against the wall at the bar with my greasy sunburned head lighting up the corner. I was the new face so I put up with the looks that I tried to avoid. The bartender in the morning just looked like a wino who worked for drinks. The girl who would normally work the tables was pretty enough. She was sweeping up last nights broken glass and cigarette butts. There was even blood on the floor in one spot and she swept over it as if it wasn't there. I guess the mop came out next. Playing stupid and flirting my hardest, I asked her when the place came to life. She wasn't buying any of the flirting. That meant she was a "somebody" who already *had* somebody. Her reply was a cold "Six-thirty."

I told her that she missed a spot just to be as rude as she was. Then I said, "See you later." I expected a fight later, no big thing. I knew that she hated me now and she'd be the one causing the fight. I don't like to fight, but when I'm doing it I really get involved. My father taught me not to fight to lose. In some fights, losing could mean death. Most bars came equipped with movable barstools and some of them still used big glass ashtrays, not to mention a pool table with sixteen balls and several cue sticks. Marques of Queensbury rules don't apply in bar fights.

Six-thirty would come soon enough. Right now I wanted to take Trouble for a ride and let him do some running. Then I wanted to stop by the bridge to see what was going on. The old Lonesome was spitting up its secrets.

. . .

I picked up the dog and went north of town, sort of exploring. About a half of a mile out of town, I turned into a well-used dirt road that split off going northwest. I was looking for a dirt road where people were scarce so I could let Trouble run loose.

About two miles out, I passed a private road going due west. It had a fancy but sturdy gate, which was closed and locked. I figured that the mayor lived out there. After the gated road, there were plenty of side roads to choose from. We headed east to avoid the flood plain and all the venomous snakes. I didn't want my doggie getting killed.

The woods were much thinner here and the sun made it through. There was an open sandy area at the end of this road that probably turned into a pond after a heavy rain. I parked and let Trouble out. He ran around like a puppy. I chased him around until he wore me out. I wished that I'd brought the Frisbee. The dog was nearly as tired as I was, so it was probably for the best that I hadn't.

On the way back, a car was coming out of the private road. The car looked like a Jaguar. The tall stranger was more intent on locking the gate than waving a friendly hello, which he sure as Hell didn't. Trouble was going crazy in the cab. The man at the gate never looked up. So much for the mayor or whoever it was. I'm sure that the dog was trying to tell me to watch out for that fellow. I committed his license plate number and face to memory. I was sure that I would be seeing that guy at the bar tonight. I wish I could bring Trouble. The gun would make the difference between life and death.

I took the dog home and went out by the bridge. The dredging operation was still going strong. Steve was out of shouting distance, so I honked the horn and waved. He motioned me over. I shut off the truck and walked toward him.

When I finally got to within conversation distance, Steve shouted above the machinery, "We're finding more bones as we move down. I have a total of seven adults. It's hard to tell. Most are pretty well digested. The current moved the bones up against this wall before the second bend. It's fairly deep here. Other than the one skull with the bullet hole, the remains show no signs of man made violence. That means strangulation, or they were thrown in alive. I hate to think it might be the latter, but it is certainly a possibility."

"Is the Sheriff aware of these new findings?" I asked.

Steve said that they were in constant radio contact. He also said that Jim wanted me to call in. I had almost forgotten that I was a cop.

Jim had to realize that a police radio in a bar is pretty conspicuous. He'd have to get used to using my cell phone. I waved goodbye and poked my way back to the truck with my stick.

As soon as I got away from the noise of the machinery, I called the station. My call was transferred to the Sheriff's office where Jim started in on my not checking in. I gave him my cell phone number and explained about a cop radio in the bars. He readily grasped the logic and said that he would commit my number to memory as well as program it into his cell phone. I briefed him on most of last night's activities and all of today's. He said to be careful and to carry my pistol. That made me feel better that he approved of my concealed weapon. He also told me to call the station if I was in a bind. Solemnly, he said, "Good luck and watch your back".

I went to lunch after that and had a chef's salad knowing that I'd be starving in an hour. Those vegetables never filled me up for very long, even if I ate half the rolls. That's all right, I was going to take Peg out for dinner when she got out of school. This deal with the mounting pile of bones in the river was bothering me. There were monsters among us and I had to deal with them. The tough part was that the monsters were disguised as humans.

I called Peg's house to find out what time she was expected home and invited her parents too. I had to meet them sooner or later. Her mom sounded nice on the phone. The dad would be home from work about the same time as Peggy. We'd meet at 5:15 at their place. I'd be sure to wear something besides jeans and a T-shirt.

I played a little Frisbee with Trouble before I showered. Then I put on some black pants and a powder blue shirt. I even shined my shoes. I fed the dog before getting in the pickup and heading for Peggy's house.

When I got there, Peggy came running out and jumped into my arms. [Some women have no taste in men.] Her parents were a little more reserved even though they greeted me warmly. Neither one jumped into my arms. Her dad, Bob, came right to the point. "Peggy says that you're the one. She's young and eager. Treat her with respect." He said it like an order rather than a request.

Her mom, Lil, was equally concerned but not as gruff as Bob. If Bob knew me better, he would have more respect. I could teach him some, but he might turn out to be family.

After dinner I told Bob that I had business at Mike's bar outside of town and asked if he would help me to convince Peg that it was too rough for a lady. Peggy spoke up and said that she already knew and would I please not go so I didn't get hurt. Again I repeated my speech about not worrying about me so much as the rest of the world.

Bob offended me for the last time when he said that a brave speech doesn't replace brave deeds. First I told him about my job as Point Man in Vietnam, then I picked him up by the waist over my head and told him that he couldn't handle my job. When I set him back down, he tried to disarm the situation by saying that Peggy had found a man this time. At least he made it clear that we could still get along despite our differences.

We went in two vehicles so I would be able to go straight to the bar and have more time to get settled at Mike's Place. After dinner I hugged Peg and said goodbye to all. I felt bad about humiliating Bob like that, but I had taken all that I was going to take. Maybe it was a deliberate test. At any rate it was water under the bridge now.

I went home and changed into jeans and a shirt so tight that I could hardly pull it down. Might as well put my politics up front. People tend to underestimate me in baggy clothes.

The trip out to Mike's Place was full of expectancy. I didn't 'expect' to meet Mr. Big tonight, but I did 'expect' to fight one or more of his men. My bare head was golden brown now instead of that embarrassing shade of shiny red. It was 6:45 PM. I suspected that the barmaid was already getting some gorilla all worked up about me. The place was still pretty empty. Gorgeous was in a conversation with the bouncer. They shut up when I came in, how obvious. I went to the stool by the wall so I would have no blind spots. I got a draught beer and leaned against the wall watching the bouncer in the mirror.

He was aware of the mirror trick and our eyes met. Neither of us would blink. The barmaid was chattering away. My phone was on my belt, my gun was in my pocket, my anger was on my sleeve and my temper floated over my head like a dark cloud. When the bouncer started moving my way I hopped off the stool and started walking right at him. When he was almost in my kill zone, I asked, "Are you lookin' for somethin'?"

" I need to know who you are," he said.

"Take one step closer and you will definitely find out!" I told him. That really pushed him over the edge. When he moved at me, I dropped and did a leg sweep on him. I stamped on both of his ankles before he could regain his feet. Now he couldn't stand. I took the phone off my belt and dialed 911 asking for an ambulance to come to Mike's. They said that they knew where it was. So now it was in the open. The short, bald headed stranger was trouble in spades. I went to sit back in my corner and ordered a shot to go with my beer. At least I wasn't cut off. He poured my shot and gave me a grin. The barmaid was furious and wasn't keeping it a secret. Hell, it was out of her hands now. I tossed down my shot and went back to the bouncer. "I'm sorry that we couldn't have met under different circumstances. I apologize for breaking your ankles. It was the only way to beat you short of a bullet."

He replied, "Well hell, thanks for not shooting me." That had us both laughing. I told him to roll onto the stretcher when it came to avoid further injury to his ankles. Then I went back to my corner.

The place gradually filled up as the ambulance arrived. I went to the bouncer and we exchanged names. Tim was his name but everyone called him Bear. I told him that I would teach him that move when he was feeling up to it. I supported his legs when he rolled onto the stretcher so he wouldn't bump his broken ankles. He was sweating, but he took the pain well.

Moving back to the bar, I could see that now there was a very sexy and pretty girl sitting next to my stool. I sipped my draught and watched the mirror. This girl was either sent to gather information, or she, too, has lousy taste in men. It's not like she had no other choice of seats. There were other seats at the bar and most of the tables were open.

She started the inevitable conversation by saying that nobody had ever whipped Bear before. I said that I was sorry to have to do it, and went back to my drink. She was determined to talk and asked me my name. I gave it to her in exchange for hers, which she claimed was "Sue".

I couldn't read her. She may have been a violence groupie or another player looking for answers. If I took it slowly, I might learn more than her. I made it a point never to assume that a person is stupid or honest. We talked a little about nothing in particular. She asked me where I worked. I used the name of my last employer. Then she asked what brought me to this nasty bar. I told her that its reputation had me curious. "I have more fun in the rough places because the girls are always prettier," I said.

"Thank you," she replied with a beautiful and disarming smile. She had taken my remark as the compliment that it was intended to be.

I bought her the obligatory drink. She didn't ask any more questions. Maybe my name was all that she was supposed to get. Maybe she just wanted to meet me. Soon the jukebox was so loud that talking was out of the question. She stayed by me and nursed her drink.

I figured that she was low on funds and didn't want to order another. So like a gentleman, I asked her if she'd like another on me.

"Thank you" she said, ordering another after she drained the last of her glass and handed it to the bartender. When he came back, she gave me another genuinely nice smile. I actually thought that she liked me which would be a shame.

By now the bar was packed and the tables were filling up. I told her that I'd take her to a table but I wanted my back to the wall, besides, I didn't trust the barmaid. Sue said that I was smart not to trust her. She said that Alice, the barmaid, had gotten a lot of guys beaten up by Bear. So Bear wasn't 'Mr. Congeniality'. Maybe he was just so wrapped up in Alice that he'd do anything to please her. Girls like that aren't capable of love. Tim was wasting his time. There was a broken heart in his future if he loved her.

Now I asked her a question, "What time does the boss get in?" That didn't even ruffle her feathers. She said that he was usually here by ten. I really didn't want to wait that long but it was my job. I had to establish if the boss of Mike's was Mr. Big or just another member of the cast. I told Sue that I'd keep her glass full if she would introduce me to the owner. She said that Mike was an evil man. He might be angry about Bear's ankles. I suggested that I could bounce until Tim had recuperated. That might make him less angry. She agreed but said that she couldn't help me if Mike got mad. So maybe Mike was Mr. Big himself. All that I could do was hope.

Sue was glad for a full glass but she wasn't getting drunk or taking advantage of my generosity. When I was done with this zoo, I was honestly going to miss her. Alice was so cocky that she was probably involved more deeply than just sweeping floors.

At precisely ten o'clock, a tall, bald headed man strode in. It was the man that Trouble had barked at who was locking the gate. I guessed him for Mike. Alice immediately went up to him and started talking. I knew that I was the subject of their conversation because he kept looking at me and nodding as she spoke. He didn't look the least bit afraid, only interested. I wanted to show that I wasn't afraid either so I had Sue come with me for the introduction. She stood a little behind me and spoke in a small, frightened voice. After she'd made her introduction, she went back and sat on her stool, watching us from the mirror.

Mike and I were staring at each other's eyes, which will start a fight anywhere. Without looking away, he asked, "Who is supposed to work the door with Bear laid up?"

Still looking in his eyes, I told him, "I'll do it for free until Tim comes back."

His answer was, "I'll shake on that."

When I shook his hand, it was like touching a snake, a poisonous one. He had big, strong hands. I had the feeling that he could whip Bear, head on, no tricks. Mike was a scary dude.

I gave him my cell phone number. This was new technology for these bumpkins, but Mike took it in stride. I guess that he got out more than most people around here. I realized that I hadn't made a new friend, this was strictly business. So I took up the perch at the door, and didn't look at Mike anymore. I had to play low key to avoid suspicion. At closing time there were no fights to break up. People were in awe of the stranger at the door and must have sensed Mike's uneasiness at the awkward situation.

I asked Sue if she needed a ride. She thanked me and said that she already had one.

When Mike approached the door, I asked him the show up time for the doorman. He said, "Six PM."

I hopped off the stool and walked to my truck. I never looked back or said goodnight. We knew that we weren't friends or anything like it.

I drove home knowing that I was being followed. I parked the truck and waved at the car pulling up to the curb across the street. I walked to my door and let Trouble loose in the front yard. He put his paws up on the fence and growled at the car across the street. It pulled a 'U' turn, and as they drove by, the dog barked savagely. I waved again but the tinted windows could have hidden anything.

My phone was ringing now. It was Peggy wanting to know if I wanted company.

"Sure do," I replied. She said that she would be there in five minutes. I sat on the steps with Trouble at my side waiting for Peg to show. The phone rang again. It was Jim. I asked him what he was doing up so late.

"Waiting for that zoo to close so I could call you," he said. I filled him in as Peggy came up the walk. Trouble didn't even bark. So now I had three employers and I was still going to sleep late tomorrow.

I told Peggy about my job at Mike's Place and informed her, "The hours are six PM 'til closing. I can see you after school until about quarter to six. I forgot to ask if there were any days off. I'll find that out tomorrow. When the smoke clears, I'll tell you everything. Come inside Sugar and bring your toothbrush if you brought one."

As soon as Peggy left for school the following morning, I phoned the station. Jim Goodson agreed to meet me at the bridge after breakfast. I told him not to approach me if he saw anything suspicious and I would do the same. I arrived first without being followed. Looking around, I saw nothing to make me apprehensive. I looked under the bridge too just in case. I already knew that it was a good hiding place. The dredge was on the south side of the river checking for remains against that rock wall. Steve was back at his post raking through the mud. I could see more human bones piling up behind him. I wondered if Bear had created any of those bodies. I'm sure that Mike had. Wrapping up this case would take quite a while waiting for the identification of all those bones. Who is to say that all the dead were local or even U.S. citizens. I imagine tourists from other countries as well as the bumper crop of illegal aliens could very well supply victims.

A car was coming from the direction of Granger. It turned out to be my friend the Sheriff. Jim parked by the other vehicles and got out. He ignored me at first, watching the operation with binoculars. When he dropped the binoculars, he gave me a quick nod and I walked over to him. I told him that if a car came from either direction that I would leave. He said that the estimate on the raft today was about thirty victims up to now.

He already knew my suspicions about Mike. I asked him where Mike lived. He said, "At the end of that private road with the fancy locked gate."

"Do you think that the tavern business would support that style of life?" I asked him.

Jim said that he had never driven down the private road before, but he had flown over it one sunny day. "The house was bigger than any on the square in town. There were several vehicles on the property. Most of them were fancy and foreign. There is a huge swimming pool and clothes weren't in fashion. Everyone waved at the plane like they were proud to be seen in their birthday suits. I never flew over again, but we need to find out what goes on inside the house and who all is involved, and no, I don't think that tavern owners made enough to live in that style."

I went back to the house to pick up Trouble and do some exploring. That abandoned dirt road going west of town seemed like a good start. The dog seemed to know that we were on an adventure. We drove through the treacherous loose sand about a mile and a half to the river. There used to be a bridge here. I guess that taxpayers can't support a road to nowhere even if it was a short cut to nowhere. I figured that it would meet Main Street eventually. Without a boat, I wouldn't think of crossing that river. The water was murky here like something was always stirring up the bottom and there was a good crop of seaweed like most of the rest of the river. Trouble and I played Frisbee in the sand. My shirt was draped over the steering wheel drying out while my bald and I head got more tanned. After awhile, I grabbed a chunk of driftwood and walked down to the river. I started moving the seaweed away so Trouble could get a drink.

When it seemed safe I called the dog so he could drink. Even the dog was nervous and watchful. He could probably smell the alligator's breath hanging above the water. We both backed away from the water like the dog could read the same danger that I perceived. We turned around to climb the little hill and upon looking back, I could see the eyes and snout of a real monster of an alligator poked up where I had moved the seaweed. Perfect timing, God was watching over us. The beast stayed in the water and eventually sunk out of sight. The second bit of good news was that there were no bodies around either.

There would have to be some other way to spy on Mike's house. I even contemplated a high powered telescope from the water tower in Granger. I guess it was a good time to check with the FBI.

We rode back to my house. I put Trouble in the front yard. I called the number that was given for the local FBI office. My contact was a man named Harold. That is exactly who answered the phone. I told him everything I knew and suspected including the possibility of foreigners among the victims. Then I told him of the dilemma that I had trying to spy on the big house.

"No problem," said Harold, "I'll rappel some men out there tonight with telescopes and listening devices. They can also place live cameras on the driveway so we can run all the license plates."

"What if they have dogs?" I asked.

"Then we give them bacon laced with a powder that puts them to sleep for a while, or we shoot them with a tranquilizer dart" said Harold.

I thanked him for the prompt service as a courtesy. We both knew that I had my neck stuck out the farthest.

I went to the local diner for a late lunch. One of the waitresses looked an awful lot like Sue. I asked to be seated in her section. The place was pretty empty, so talking should be easier. After I had ordered my meal, I asked the girl if she had a sister.

"Yes, her name is Suzanne," she told me.

Then I asked if she and her sister had spoken lately. She told me that they roomed together. Liz, my waitress, said that Sue had awakened her last night to talk. "Before you go any farther, you should know that my name is Al Benson."

"Holy cow, you beat up Bear?" she asked incredulously. "You know that Sue is crazy about you. She said that you scared her because you got in Mike's face. She thinks you're nuts! She said that you're the bouncer there until Tim is back on his feet."

"Unfortunately all of that is true. That bar is so crazy, you never know who your friends are and you never know who has guns." She hurried to place my order on the wheel, coming back with a coffee pot and a cup.

She told me that Sue was afraid that Mike would kill me when Bear got back. I told her that people have been trying to kill me on and off for years. Each day was like the rest, stay alert, stay alive, and trust in The Lord.

With a steaming cup of coffee in front of me, the world seemed a little farther away. If you can't push your troubles aside every now and then, they will scare you to death or eat you up with ulcers.

After lunch I went home to take a nap before work. I let Trouble in where he followed me around until I lay down. He curled up on the floor next to the bed and we both passed out.

I awoke to a knocking at the door. Peggy was home from school. It was 4 o'clock. I let her in and told her that I'd have to take a shower. She said that she'd wait. When I came out with a towel on, I was over-dressed for the occasion. I slipped into something more comfortable.

. . .

Later, we talked about what went on last night at Mike's. Peggy said that she was afraid for my safety. "Don't even go back," she said.

I reminded her that it was part of my job, period. "I have accepted responsibility and money to get something done. Besides, if I don't go back, Mike will try to get me killed. If it happened when you and me were together, you or both of us might get killed." Then I took out my .38 special and told her that I was authorized to use it at my discretion.

"This gun goes everywhere with me. It was with me last night and I never needed it. Now you have to go home and I have to go to work." I kissed her goodbye wondering if she would tell her parents and hoping she wouldn't.

I got to Mike's at straight up six o'clock and had a seat at the door. The place was pretty empty. Alice the bitch was there. She was putting big glass ashtrays on all the tables. I'd have to talk to Mike about getting them switched to something less lethal. The bartender looked up and grinned. He might be all right. It was too soon to tell. When Alice worked her way over to me, she totally ignored me. People like her hold a grudge. She would probably try something else tonight. I asked her as politely as I could if Tim was feeling better, but got no reply. Well, at least she knew that I was still alive.

People eventually started showing up. I hadn't had much of a chance to study the patrons last night. They were a motley bunch. The skinny ones in long sleeve shirts were the needle freaks. They shot anything and everything. If they were at the pool table, it was probably speed in one form or another. The ones nodding out at the bar were the heroin addicts. The ones constantly going in and out were the pot-heads or dealers. You could tell by whom they went out with what that particular person was selling.

There was a hard-core group of evil looking bikers who sat by themselves. Alice seemed to know this bunch. Either that or she was getting to know them. It really didn't matter to me and I think that she hated me more for my indifference.

Finally Sue showed up. She said hello, but I could tell that she didn't want to hang around the door. I smiled and said to stick to the corner where I could see her. If some other handsome devil goes over by you, I won't wring his neck or break his ankles unless you scream. She smiled again and headed straight for the seat that I asked her to.

I hated the fact that she really liked me. That could make complications later. If it wasn't for the fact that Peggy was just as cute, I'd be buying flowers for Sue. Another thing in Peggy's favor was that she would never come in a bar like this more than one time.

The joint was packed now and getting loud. Someone stuffed a couple dollars into the jukebox and it actually seemed quieter. At least the din had rhythm now. My phone rang. I covered one ear to hear better. It was Mike asking how things were going and telling me that he'd be there in ten minutes. He hung up without saying goodbye. I owed him for that. He'd get as much respect as he gave out and that was none.

In ten minutes, Mr. Big walked in. I stifled the hello that he expected. I didn't even look at him. Hell, I was working. Two men at the pool table were obviously fixing to throw down on each other. I walked over and told them that they couldn't fight inside and if they fought outside, they weren't allowed back in. Now they were mad at me and forgot about their personal feud. When I turned around, Mike was standing in my way. He said that I handled that very diplomatically and much better than Bear would have. Then he surprised me by moving out of my way, allowing me to pass.

My radar was spinning rapidly. I didn't believe his show of gratitude and hospitality. The four bikers looked like they were leaving. I smelled four rats. I went to a couple of tables and grabbed the ashtrays. Then I resumed my position at the door as the snakes approached. I hopped down with an ashtray in each hand. "Goodnight gentleman, please come again."

Everyone read the ashtrays. Now they spread out in a four-man front. Gentlemen, don't do anything foolish. I dropped an ashtray so my right hand was free. Then I fished out the .38 special so the butt was showing. "Whatever you're getting paid ain't worth your lives."

All four made a move that could only be interpreted as drawing a gun. I couldn't wait. I drew the revolver and made every shot a kill. I took two bullets, non-lethal wounds, but they still hurt. Two of them were jerking in their death throes, goners despite the signs of vitality.

I got out the cellular phone and dialed 911. The Sheriff himself picked up immediately.

"I've been shot at Mike's Place. I'll live, but I got four stiffs on the floor. Send an ambulance with the cavalry." In minutes I could hear sirens. Jim was first through the door followed by four uniforms.

"Who saw the actual shootings?" asked the Sheriff. Sue was the first one to come forward. Mike admitted that he had too. Alice just hung in the back ground seething with anger.

"He shot in self defense," Sue volunteered. "The other men drew their guns on him."

Jim told them to wait outside. "I'll need to take a statement from each of you. Jim took my gun and picked up the other four by the barrels.

When the ambulance showed, Jim cuffed me to the gurney saying, "I'll have to hold you for awhile." The paramedics started on me right away. The uniforms stayed with the bodies until the Coroner's hearse showed up. God only knew what could be found by searching them.

Sue rode to the station in Jim's car. The Sheriff told Mike to come in at his earliest convenience. I went to the local doctor who removed the bullets and did a little extra first aid. Before he released me, he wrote a prescription for painkillers and another for antibiotics. Fortunately, the bullets that hit me were only .32 caliber. No organs had been hit according to the doctor. Once again, The Lord had been looking out for me.

I walked back to the police station under escort looking like "The Mummy" from the waist up. Jim and Sue were there. Sue gave me a kiss on the cheek. Jim gave me back my gun in front of her, which I didn't think was a good idea. I assumed that the Sheriff knew her better than either one let on.

"Alfred, you're remarkable. First you whip Tim the Bear, then beat those four. You are cleaning up the dirty end of Dodge." Jim said that in the morning, he would check fingerprints on the other guns. "You might have to stay the night in the city jail, just for show."

I told him that someone had to retrieve my truck from the bar and I had to feed the dog and let him out. Then I could be his guest.

I rode in the back of the squad for appearances. Sue rode in front so she could drive my truck back. The bar was still hopping. Mike was sitting on the stool inside the open door. He stood up long enough to take in the scene. He walked over to the squad and asked Jim if bail could be set. Sheriff Goodson said that I would be freed in the morning if the fingerprints told the same story as their statements. Mike waved at me as the unmarked vehicle pulled out followed by Sue in my truck. Jim drove Sue home while I sat in jail. When he came back, he cuffed my hands in front and we fed the dog and let him out. Trouble looked incredulous to see me leave.

I called Peggy and asked her to come by the station. She was shocked to see me behind bars and covered with bandages. When I clued her in, she felt much better. I showed her my .38 and asked her how many criminals were allowed to keep their gun and cell phone behind bars. Then I gave her my keys and asked if she'd mind staying with Trouble until school time in the morning. She agreed without a problem. I thanked her and said goodnight.

· · ·

I wasn't happy to be in jail, but I was in better shape than those four bikers were. I was sore and in some pain when I sat up. The first thing that I did was to call over to Peggy's house to see how she had gotten along with Trouble. Her mom said that Peggy had taken Gladys over to my house and her daughter was in the shower. Lil said that the dogs got on well and that her daughter had left Gladys over at my house. I told her to have Peggy call me before she left.

Next I called Harold at the FBI to see if last night's mission had been carried out. He said that the place had more bugs than the Kremlin and more cameras than Hollywood. "We have so many men out there that Mike's house is virtually surrounded. Mike didn't have any dogs which made everyone's job easier."

Then I told him that I had been shot twice and spent the night in jail. "You what?" I gave him a brief account of last night's adventure. Then I told him that I had to clear the line for another call.

It was Peggy on call waiting. She wanted to know how I felt and if I'd be out that afternoon. I told her that I was feeling OK and would definitely be out this afternoon. Then I called the Sheriff at his desk and told him to come see me. He walked back to the holding cell and said, "What now?" in a jokingly gruff manner.

I asked him what was a realistic time for the evidence technicians to get prints from the stiffs and match them to the guns. He said that I'd be out at ten o'clock at the latest if that had been my intended question.

"How about some breakfast?" I asked. He promised to call across the street and pick it up personally. I gave him my order and asked if he had the prescriptions filled yet. The antibiotics were very important.

The Sheriff sent a deputy to pick up the prescriptions while he went for breakfast. There were Coroner's assistants in the basement and dispatch was sitting at the front desk. You could almost hear a pin drop for a while. Then I heard voices up front. The dispatcher came and opened the door to tell me that I had a visitor.

Mike strolled into the room. "May we speak in private?" he asked in a voice that would melt butter. The dispatcher left us alone.

Mike started off; "You're fast, smart and deadly. I happen to have an opening nearer the top of my organization. It pays better than what you're accustomed to. There are also fringe benefits. My house is always filled with pretty girls. We already use the same hairdresser, so why not join my staff?"

"Let me get out of here first, then I'll gladly join you. I know that it was you who sent those bikers to kill me, so I'll be watching you. If I feel trapped, I'll shoot you first," I said.

Not addressing my point blank accusation, he agreed and said that pay starts at a grand per week.

"See me at the bar tonight at ten o'clock. There will be a new man at the door. You'll never have to sit there again," he said. Then we shook hands and he left as the Sheriff was walking in with my breakfast. They nodded to each other. No smiles, only respect due to sworn enemies.

I told Jim, "I don't know if I can trust him or not, but Mike offered me a promotion. I'll be getting one large per week as pay for doing God knows what. Also, he said that he got a new bouncer."

"Take the job and see where it leads." That was the last thing that he said until after breakfast. When he finally spoke, he said that it was a good thing that I was locked up when Mike dropped in. Forensics finally showed up with the good news that the prints on the four guns matched one each of the dead men. So I was a free man.

I reminded Jim to stay in touch with the FBI and told him that Harold had several men on the property already. Then I called Harold and told him of my elevated status. All that he said was to be careful. "I got shot twice last night and I killed four men. How does one be careful when dealing with this man?"

It was silent on his end for a while. When he finally spoke, I could hear the hopefulness coming through the wires. "You can retire now if you want to, but you're already our most valuable man in the operation."

I told him that it was no worse than Vietnam. "Let's wrap this up before more bodies are created." I took my pills before I left the station to walk home. My truck was parked in the street and I had two dogs in my front yard. Gladys took to me like family. Praise the Lord, it was safe to walk in my own yard. I let the dogs in and slept for a while.

Taking a shower was a real trip with all the bandages on my upper torso. I finally gave up and filled the tub for a bath. I brought the gun and cell phone in the bathroom out of force of habit.

When I was as clean as I could get, I toweled off and dressed to the best of my ability. By the time I was done bathing, I was hurting pretty badly despite having taken a painkiller earlier. I figured that the bandages would serve as my shirt. The doctor could change them tomorrow.

I fed the dogs before letting them in the back yard. They chased each other around like newly weds.

Peggy showed up and made a big deal over my injuries. I soaked it up. After all, I could have been killed. We sat in the sun in the back yard and watched the dogs play.

I told Peg about my offer from Mike and the request from the FBI. I also told her my response and my true feelings why.

I warned her that she, or one of her friends, could be among the next bodies in the Lonesome. I also told her that the FBI had men on the property to make it a little safer for me. I broke down and told her that I was a county cop under cover and on loan to the FBI who was also paying me. I told her that I had a place in Smallville where she would be welcome with her dog.

"For now, you can't tell anyone, not even your parents", I warned. I told her of my meeting with Mike tonight at ten. We went inside where she promised to help me get dressed again when we were through.

Ten o'clock was nearing. Peg tied my boots for me. I asked her to stay, saying that I would be back around midnight. "Do your homework," I suggested. Then I got in my truck and headed to Mike's. I beat him by a few minutes.

The new gorilla at the door looked big enough to be dangerous, but if brains were dynamite, he probably couldn't blow his nose. I'm sure that he wasn't in the inner loop. At any rate, he paid no attention to my entry. Probably some ex-con that needed a job. I nodded to Sue but I didn't sit by her. I found a corner table where Mike usually hung out.

I had just ordered a shot and a beer when Mike walked in. He spotted my bald head right away and came over smiling. Somehow a smile looked out of place on him. Still, I returned it. As usual, we shook hands and then he sat down. "That's a hell of a shirt, Alfred. I hope that it doesn't hurt too much." I had a feeling that Mike didn't have any friends and maybe he was soliciting me for that exalted position.

He sat next to me with his back to the other wall in the corner. "Al, I need a personal bodyguard. I'm surrounded with people whom I can no longer trust. The men that you killed last night were to fill that position. You saved me a lot of money last night and into the future. Keep your revolver, but let me give you a gift. The time may come when you will need more than six bullets." He placed an expensive looking fourteen shot semiautomatic pistol on the table with a box of fifty rounds and a couple of extra magazines.

I thanked him profusely and checked out my new toy. He said that the fewer bodies, the better, but he had a dumping ground that was infallible. I'm aware of all the bodies tossed in the river. Those bodies had nothing to do with me. That is how amateurs do things. Finish your drink and we'll go for a ride."

Tonight he was driving a Jaguar with tinted windows. "This thing has a modified engine that will take it up to 200 miles per hour. I have never had to use that feature, but it's there. Would you like to drive?"

"Sure, I said." He tossed the keys to me and climbed into the passenger side.

We were alone in the car. That was a relief. Either he trusted me or he was going to kill me himself. I preferred to think that it was trust. He steered me out to the private road with the gate. He got out and did his thing with the key, making sure to lock it once I was inside with the car.

"Al, this is another world you're in now. I make the rules. You will meet people here that you would see in few other locations on the planet. Some if not all of those people covet what I have going out here. Between the two of us, we'll ferret out the dangerous ones and trim fat where necessary. Keep your guns ready and your eyes open. If someone makes you uncomfortable, push the matter and kill him if you have to. First there is a movie that I'd like for you to see."

We passed through the great room, which was full of strangers, mostly attractive women. They were Playboy Bunny materiel. Then he showed me his other pool, the much larger, indoor one. There were several well-fed alligators inside with a four-foot tall cyclone fence around it. All of the 'gators were ten feet or more. There was an extremely tall cherry picker in the corner of the room. It was tall enough to put engines in small airplanes.

Now we entered another room that looked like a theater, he started up a large screen television and turned off the lights by remote. The scene on the DVD that Mike played was filmed in the room that we just left. There was a local cop laughing and joking with Mike and Bear. They were the only three people in the room at this time.

The cop acted like he didn't have a worry in the world. Then Bear hit him from behind. The cop dropped like a rock. The sound was as clear as the picture. Mike and Bear spun a few loops of nylon rope around the cop's ankles and tied a square knot. The cable from the cherry picker was hooked to the rope and the man was lifted upside down and swung over the pool. Mike walked out of the room briefly and came back with several people of both sexes. Bear shook up a beer and sprayed the cop until he came to. When the cop realized his predicament, he started pleading for his life.

The people outside the fence were of mixed emotions. Some were making fun of the cop. Some were laughing. Some left the room, but very few. Bear started lowering the hapless man into the water. The Mike in the film responded like the Mike in the room with me, with kind of an insane chuckle. The look on his face now was one of rapture. He truly enjoyed every minute of it. He took over the crank from Bear and lowered the cop to within inches of the water.

One of the smaller alligators sprung up and managed a bite of the cop's face before the bigger ones rushed over and drove him off. Mike raised him again. The man was filling the pool with blood and screaming incoherently, completely hysterical. Then Mike lowered him so his head was almost completely submerged. He still screamed and tried beating the alligators away with his fists. The 'gators were now ripping at his arms. Mike cranked him up again so everyone could see the damage. A few more people left at this point.

The cop's head was gone and the arms were grotesque, bloody stumps. Mike raised him and swung him back on this side of the fence. He stripped the hideous piece of meat of anything that might harm the alligators. Then he swung him back over the fence and cut the nylon rope.

"I could watch that movie a hundred times and still get a kick out of it," Mike chuckled.

"Hell, play it again. I ain't heard screams like that since Vietnam. War is the ultimate adventure and I loved it. I never thought I would die until I started walking point on a permanent basis. Then I thought that every step would be my last. That's a hell of a rush. That's where I learned to be fast and deadly," I told him with as much sincerity as I could muster. "That was obviously a crooked cop. What did he do to wind up like hamburger?" I asked like it was no big thing.

"He asked for a raise," Mike said, thoroughly convinced that he needed no better reason.

"So, let's rewind it," I said. We watched it again. This time I concentrated on the faces in the audience while Mike sat next to me, chuckling all along. He and this whole bunch belonged in hell. I was determined to send them there.

After the show, Mike gave me a key to the gate. He asked if I were coming back tonight. I said, "Not tonight." I told him that I had a date later and a doctor's appointment in the morning. I told him that the Sheriff ruled the four stiffs as justifiable homicide so there wouldn't be any expensive lawyers to worry about. Then I asked for a ride to my truck.

On the way to my vehicle, he said that he needed me to start as soon as possible. "Tomorrow night I can start full time." I said. "As a matter of fact, I can stay with you until 11:30 tonight if you want some company."

"That would be great," he said. So we went back to his tax front "Mike's Place" and whiled away an uneventful evening.

. . .

I got home at 11:45. The dogs greeted me at the door but Peggy was sound asleep. I slipped in beside her and lay down to sleep. The alarm went off at 11:55 and scared the hell out of me. Peg freaked when she saw me already there. "How did you get in here without waking me?" she asked.

I told her that the dogs didn't bark and the rest was easy. I clued her in on tonight's happenings sparing her the details of the movie. I told her that I was a thousand dollar per week bodyguard for the owner of Mike's. The problem was that I'd be sleeping at the mansion at the end of the private road. She wasn't happy at all to hear that.

"Alfred, those people are awful. Be careful," she said. Then I showed her the 9mm semi-auto and said that it was a gift from Mike. Tomorrow morning I was going to test fire it at the dead end road with the bridge out.

"Peggy," I said, "I'm the best man for this job and I think I can pull it off. Don't forget that there is already an FBI presence out there. They have body armor and automatic rifles, not to mention telescopes, cameras, and listening devices. Those guys have more training than I do. Hopefully, they're not a bunch of cherries."

"What are cherries?" Peggy asked.

"Cherries are what we call soldiers or policemen who haven't been in gunfights or killed anyone. Until the stuff hits the fan, you never know who can handle it or who will freeze or who will run. Let's make tonight a good one since it may have to last us for a week or two." It was 3 AM before we got to sleep.

She left for school in the morning. I gave instructions on feeding Trouble and told her that she could leave Gladys here if she wanted.

I went to the river, alone this time. The 9mm worked fine. It fitted my hand nicely too. I liked the idea of carrying two guns anyway.

It was time for my doctor's appointment. I grabbed a nice looking long sleeved white shirt to wear over the clean bandages I'd be getting. The doctor was surprised at how fast I was healing. The nurse had cut away the old bandages and swabbed the wounds with hydrogen peroxide. The nurse gave my upper body a sponge bath. That was the best I could do to clean my upper body. I could shampoo in my kitchen sink and sit up in the bathtub.

When I was done at the doctors, I went home and did exactly that. Afterwards, I called Jim and Harold to update them. They said that things were moving a little fast and to proceed with caution. I told them that caution was my new middle name. I slipped on some loose fitting gray slacks and went out the door.

I drove out to the private road and let myself in, being careful to lock the gate behind me. As I went up the drive I looked for the FBI and saw no trace. Everything was as it should be. Even the cameras were invisible. Harold sent me some good men.

As I neared the outdoor pool, I could see that it was full of female revelers sans clothing and about a half dozen men. The scenery was great, but my business was with Mike and he wasn't out here. I returned the waves and let myself inside. There was no sign of Mike among the people in the great room so I asked the first smile where he was to be found. The smile stayed and the girl said that Mike was busy in his room. I asked her if she'd mention that Al Benson would be outside when he was through.

"You're Al?" She seemed surprised. "I'll be sure to tell him," she said.

Before I went out, I looked in on the alligators. Awesome beasts, was all that could be said. If the pools filter ever clogged, I wouldn't want to work on it. It must have special filtering for the alligators waste and bones that were only partially digested. I thought about that cop and got mad all over again. No one deserves to die like that.

I went out and found a seat near the pool, just far enough away to avoid getting splashed. A couple of girls came by me and asked who I was. "I'm Al Benson," I said. That triggered a ripple among all the girls. The men wouldn't look at me even though it was impossible to have missed the conversation. The crowd of girls got bigger and eventually one of the men came in front of me and said that he didn't believe that I whipped Bear or killed four armed men with four shots. I took off my shirt and told him that I was a little sore for fighting, but I would just as soon shoot him as look at him. There were too many listening to back down. The fool reached for his gun and I popped him between the eyes. "Who's next, or do I shoot the whole bunch of you now?"

Two other men made foolish moves and got a third eye. The others backed away to their chairs without looking at me. I asked the girls what Mike usually did with a mess like this. They said that he hardly ever had a mess like this outside. Feeding them to the alligators was the only suggestion offered. I said that I'd find out when he came outside.

Now I couldn't close my eyes. The other men had lost face and that is one of the wounds that pride hurts from the most. I expected a confrontation within the hour. Mike came out shortly and asked about the shooting. I told him that I had words with three of his men and things got out of hand.

Mike told the other three men to wrap them in plastic and feed the alligators. When they started to give him shit, I stood up with a gun in each hand. "Boys, have you forgotten who's boss around here? Mike runs this show and if there are any problems... Well that's where I come in and I don't like to argue. Now get some plastic and be quick about it."

After they'd gone inside, I told Mike that the shooting wasn't done. Those three are probably inside trying to recruit an army. There were four more men inside. I told the girls to move to the far side of the pool while Mike and I defended the enterprise. The women opted for leaving the pool area altogether.

We put two of the bodies in the chairs while he and I laid on the ground with a bead on the front door. We didn't have long to wait. The fools came running out the door pumping lead into the two bodies while we picked them off like flies. Mike even shot one who tried to run. I was impressed with his coolness under fire as well as his marksmanship. Now there were nine less to deal with later. Mike didn't know that he was helping the good guys.

"Hey Mike, I thought that all the alligators were in the pool," I said just to break the spell.

He grinned and said, "Now we'll have to do our own cleanup. I have a wheel barrow that will make that job easier." He knew where the plastic was and I had a knife. Before too long, we were dumping the last creep over the fence. The 'gators were in a feeding frenzy. He wouldn't have to buy any meat for a while, that is if he ever bothered to. Now, to hose down the concrete outside.

Mike said that he could have one of the girls wash me and change my bandages. That sounded pretty good after all that work. We were both covered in blood and my painkiller was wearing off. Mike said that he'd fix me up with some new clothes if I didn't mind. We would have to burn ours. I agreed to everything. He told me that we had just wiped out all his problems in one day. Now he could show me how he squeezed out the money to keep this place afloat and the taxes paid.

After we were both clean and dressed, he and I walked back to the projection room. He showed me crates of film.

"All of these are snuff films. These are the hottest thing on the international market. The more grisly the better. The ones with women in them sell the fastest. People don't want to see beautiful women wasted on alligators. Those we take care of personally after a romp in bed. Strangulation is the most popular, sometimes a slit throat. We started out doing just street corner runaways snatched from around the country. That's when I saw my pets as more than pets. They are great disposal units. We snared a few bigger ones and mixed them in with the ones I already had. They were fed so well that they grew to amazing proportions in no time."

"Some of my guys were loose cannons. They were dumping bodies unrelated to my business and now there's an investigation including a dredge at the bridge on the way to Smallville," he finished.

"I saw the dredge. Now I know why it's there." I said, just playing stupid.

Then he showed me the rest of his empire. There was a hall going off from the theater that led to a set of stairs. This place had a full basement that was also loaded with marijuana plants. A smaller part was devoted strictly as a laboratory cranking out God knows what. I finally had the whole picture. We could surround this place and close it down.

I said that I couldn't believe that I could live here with all these women and a grand per week just to be his bodyguard. Mike said to make that two large. When the street heard that there were nine less men guarding the fort, we were going to be in trouble.

"Don't tell the street and neither would I," I told him.

"What about Bear?" asked Mike.

"We'll have him move out here and then we can kill him," I said. "Then all of this will be just our secret. If you think that you can trust him, we'll just let him stay on to tend the plantation and watch our pharmacists."

"I'm the only pharmacist here," said Mike, "and I can tend the plants. I like your first idea better. You just hang around the pool and look scary and occasionally I'll let you out to spend your money. You can even bring that big dog of yours. He is very intimidating."

That remark told me that one of the passengers in the car with the tinted windows turned in an accurate report.

"I'm afraid that he wouldn't be much good out here. He would stand outside the plantation door barking. That dog used to be a police dog," I told him.

"I had great difficulty just getting him used to me. I like that animal and I would feel badly if you wound up shooting him to save your life," I said.

Mike asked, "Where did *you* get a police dog?"

I told him that I got him at the pound in Crete. He was so mean that nobody could work around him. I hated to lie but this was one of those times. Remember my mission here was to save lives, not preach the Gospel. I told him that my dog had hit it off with my girlfriend and her dog. I'd call her and say she could keep him as a going away present.

That was the end of the discussion on Trouble. I hoped that he bought my story, but this evil man was not easily read.

"Hey Mike, what do we do for food?" I asked.

Mike said, "We have kitchen staff as well as house cleaners and a handyman."

I asked him if the staff came and went, warning that they could be a security leak if any of them left the property. He assured me that the only member of the staff that came and went freely was trustworthy. "In eleven years I've had no trouble from that direction."

I suggested that we should check on lunch because I was starving. His reply was that the "fun" by the pool gave him an appetite too.

Mike's kitchen staff earned their money. They provided a gourmet feast at the snap of a finger. A man could get fat living here. "Hey Mike, does this place have a weight room?" I asked.

"Yes it does. First door on the right going up the hall. It has it's own full bath and shower. But I don't think that you should be lifting weights until your stitches are out," he said.

I agreed with him totally. I told him that I expected them out in one week since my prescriptions elapsed in one week.

"Who, besides you, me, Bear, and that member of the kitchen staff has keys to the gate?" I asked.

Mike said, "You've just named all the keys." Then I asked him where Bear was now. He said that he is in one of the back bedrooms right now. Probably being attended to by one or more of the girls.

"When the hell did he get back?" I asked.

"Tim has been here since he left the hospital, the first night you took his place at the door," Mike said, watching my eyes.

My voice had risen a decibel or two, "NO SECRETS AND NO

SURPRISES!" I practically shouted. Mike said to take it easy. He wasn't sure of me at first.

"ARE YOU SURE NOW, OR WOULD YOU LIKE YOUR KEY?" I *was* shouting now.

Then it was Mike's turn to shout, "NOBODY RAISES HIS VOICE AROUND HERE BUT ME!" I expected that reaction.

I angrily told him that no one raised *their* voice to me ever. By then, Bear was making his way into the room on crutches. He couldn't get his gun out fast enough. My new pistol was in one hand covering both of them. I dug out my cell phone and speed dialed Harold. "Send his men in one at a time right now.".

Soon there were eight of us police types making it easier to disarm Mike and Tim. They were cuffed right away. Next I called Jim and asked for a couple of uniforms and four paddy wagons. Soon the place was cleared of riffraff. I took Jim and Harold into the projection room and played the film with the cherry picker, which was still on the camera. Both men were visibly shaken by the viewing.

"These two deserve the chair. I hope like hell that they're still using Old Sparky. All the others watching can be compared to their mug shots. That should establish complicity to murder. Gentlemen, I need a rest from this place but before I go, I must show you the rest of the operation." So I showed them the indoor pot plants and the drug lab plus the library of snuff films. I told Harold that if they answered the phone here for a while, they could probably arrest a lot of customers for the films and the dope.

I asked Jim if the lock at the gate was opened. He said that bolt cutters were faster than a key. I asked for and got a week off. Then I hopped into my pick up truck and left the whole nightmare behind me until my phone should start ringing during my time off. Before I even got to the house, the phone rang. It was Harold, still back at Mike's mansion.

"Where are all the bad guys that we've been listening to?" he asked.

I told him to shoot the man-eating alligators and cut them open.

Mike and I killed nine of them this morning and dumped them in the pool.

"So that's why all the flies were hanging around the pool outside. Stay by your phone. Your vacation may have to be postponed," Harold said.

I expected it to be this way. They would have a million questions over the next few days.

When I got inside, the dogs went crazy over me. It seemed like a lifetime ago that I was leaving for Mike's mansion. After the dogs were done abusing me, I went and laid down for a nap. I hadn't even gotten to sleep when Peggy was letting herself in. Oh well, it was foolish of me to think that everyone could plan their life around me.

"Remember not to hug me too hard, the stitches are still in," I warned her. I told her that the operation was over and none of the bad guys could get off with the kind of evidence that we had on them. I told her that besides the four bikers, nine more men were killed today, and the two who were in handcuffs had no way to beat the electric chair other than suicide.

"Police work is exciting, but you meet the scummiest people, like if you x-rayed them they would show horns and a tail. I hope that all the bad guys aren't this bad. I have a week off coming soon, but I'll be attending a lot of interviews. Most of the people around here aren't aware of the bodies by the bridge. They will have a very hard time digesting the horror of the entire operation. Mike's will be raided, closed, and auctioned off. Yeah, it may be a while before I can take that week off. I will also have to make a choice between the FBI and being a Deputy Sheriff. The FBI pays better, but I think that deputies spend more time at home than FBI agents. Either way, I'm going to have to attend law enforcement classes. I'll sleep on it before I decide," I told her.

"Is there room for me in all this adventure and career choices?" asked Peggy. Her question demanded a sincere answer.

"I had hoped to move you and Gladys to my mobile home in Smallville. If you can stand me, marriage is not out of the question," I said. Then I told her that I'd killed eleven people, give or take, lately, and had been shot twice. I told her that this whole adventure started with me beating alligators off a woman's corpse at a bridge where I went just to be alone. "Now I've grown attached to you and a dog that

I don't own. Trouble is a County Police Dog. I can only hope that I can buy him."

"I'm sorry to have thought of you as selfish or shallow. I'll help you convince the Sheriff that Trouble is better off with us than languishing at the Police Pound. Meanwhile, we have some catching up to do before you pass out on me," she practically purred.

I hadn't even had time to shower before the phone rang again. It was Jim telling me, "Mike is loose and Bear is dead. I need you right now and bring your dog." I was happy to hear him infer that Trouble was mine.

I put Trouble in the cab of my truck and said goodbye to Peg. I was driving like a maniac. Most of the action was now centered around the private bridge on the road to the mansion. Jim and Harold were talking as I drove up. Pulling in, I could see two bodies on the bridge.

The story that they told me was that Bear and Mike wound up in the back of a squad instead of in a paddy wagon. The squad stopped on the bridge and the driver shot his partner. He stripped the dead cop of his gun and belt. Then he let Bear and Mike out giving Mike the extra gun and belt. That's when Mike shot Bear. The cop and Mike went under the bridge into a hidden boat. Mike shot the second cop before taking off in the boat, grabbing the second belt and revolver. He went upstream like a bat out of hell. The boat had been hiding there a long time. That man trusted no one and now he had no one to split his fortune with.

Harold said that they had a helicopter coming from Crete. Until then, he wanted me to take the dog and walk down the western shore of the Lonesome. They had another dog team coming to walk down the eastern shore. I was given a police walkie-talkie and a gallon jug of fresh water. It would be funny if Mike got shot with his own gun.

Trouble and I set off on another adventure. Mike would think about a chopper and hope for dark or hold up under cover. Cover along this river meant branches and branches meant snakes. Mike might already be dead. Oh well.

I had to remember how dangerous my foe was. He would expect pursuit and he would expect me. He would also expect the dog. He would head for cover whenever he heard any kind of aircraft. If he abandoned the boat as I expected, it would be at a place where the woods came right up to the river. He had a plan or he never would have thought to stash the boat. The terrain that I was in now was pretty much unexplored except maybe by Mike and his cop friend. I still had the 'gators and snakes to worry about along with Mike to top off the dangers.

I hadn't hunted man since 1970. It wasn't fun then and it wouldn't be fun now. He may have had camouflage clothes hidden in the boat, but I doubted it. I had a distinct advantage with Trouble at my side. Mike could counterfeit the dog with an ambush. I doubted if he had a rifle since he made such a big deal out of taking the guns and ammo from the two cops.

All these thoughts were best explored now while my quarry was far away. Soon I might be concentrating on the hunt. Ambushes are hard to spot and there were many ways to conceal them.

After walking for half of an hour, watching both shores as well as possible, I spotted something big in the water drifting in my direction.

As I drew closer, I could see that it was a small outboard sunk to the rails with only the Styrofoam keeping it afloat. There were no obvious holes so I assumed that Mike had just pulled the plug. Eventually it would make its way to the private bridge. There may be some clue in there to help us complete the puzzle.

So Mike had gone aground somewhere near. He might be hunting me for all that I knew. That would make him easier to find. It was almost dark now, making tracking more difficult. I let Trouble take the lead. Eventually I saw the place where Mike went aground. He had made some crude attempts at covering the rub from the nose of his boat.

I had the dog sniff at his footprints and told him to go get 'em. As far as I could see, the trail led directly inland. The problem with rivers is that they make so many bends, that we could come across it again at any time.

The woods here were thicker, as I predicted. He needn't worry about aerial pursuit, unless they had infrared equipment. There were bears around this part of Florida to add to the excitement. It seemed that we were on a game trail. Walking was easy and occasionally I could spot a boot print in the dim light. If there were no clouds, we could easily follow this trail. It hadn't rained in a couple of weeks. Rain would make tracking nearly impossible if Mike left the game trail. We might have to wait until morning. Here I was in jeans and a T-shirt fixin' to spend the night in the woods. Maybe Mike would surprise me and surrender. Sure, when he was out of ammo.

I liked to think that I had the advantage in the dark. My military experience had included operating in the dark. Still, there was the fact that he was ahead of me, allowing him to choose an ambush site. Truthfully, I would rather be out here with Trouble than another man. I could go on like this for two days without sleep. I wondered if Mike could stay ahead of me for two days. He was a mystery to me. We never discussed each other's past. For all I knew, he might have been a Green Beret or a Navy SEAL. I could be out-gunned and not know it until too late. I think that he had a healthy respect for me since I killed those four men in his bar. That was a close one.

We were about one mile from where we left the river. The inevitable fog filled the already dark woods. I was wishing for a long sleeved shirt right about then. My back started getting stiff. I hadn't noticed, but I had been walking bent over for a long time as I tried to see the trail with it's occasionally visible boot print. I had to wonder if he had a cell phone too and if he was going to rendezvous with someone.

All kidding aside, I had complete confidence that I would come out on top of any show down with Mike since the Lord was on my side. I gave up on trying to see anything but my dog. It was a waste of time. I could barely make out his moving tail. It was time to trust his nose and training. So far he had unerringly been on the scent as the tracks proved. Still, I had no idea of how big of a head start in time that Mike's boat had given him. I made up my mind that I was going to walk 'til I found him without rest.

I was so cold that I was walking with my arms crossed under the T-shirt. I had a gun in each hand of course. The main thought in my mind was that if the dog stopped, Mike was near. I was also thinking about the name, Lonesome River. This was one spooky place. I was hunting a brave and ruthless man. I wondered what else he might have stashed on that boat that could make my life miserable and short. I still thought that my dog would be the deciding factor in this hunt. Trouble stopped. He was at alert. Dropping to my hands and knees, I crept past the dog using the butts of the pistols like crutches. My T-shirt was dangling from my neck now.

At this level, I could see the game trail once again. About ten feet ahead, I could see something blocking the trail. Crawling carefully forward, I could make out the gun belts. All the ammo had been removed from the belt along with the pepper spray. That spray stuff was hell on bears as well as dogs. If Mike sprayed my dog, I'd be bringing his body back.

Once I had picked up the belts and shown them to Trouble, he took off again at the same ground eating pace.

I had re-adjusted my T-shirt for warmth again. So, Mike was tired and he discarded the gun belts. That was a laugh. I wasn't anywhere near tired, just chilly. I kept in as good of condition as he did and I was about ten years younger. I wondered if the bullets in Mike's pockets would make enough noise to give him away as I drew nearer.

No more stray thoughts, I had to concentrate on the dog. I couldn't risk stepping on one of his paws. He might yelp and get us both shot. I already knew that Mike was a good shot.

Those gun belts were damp and cold, as if they had lain there awhile. Still, I was sure that I was closing the gap. It was pitch black now and I walked very close to Trouble to keep from losing him. I couldn't walk along side of him. The narrowness of the game trail prohibited that. I'd make too much noise crunching the under brush. Therefore I had only the one plan to follow. I felt bad for not bringing any dog food but this was a desperate search for a dangerous man. Truthfully in all my vanity, I thought that I would have caught up to him by now. I really didn't know much about the man I was after other than the ruthlessness of his character. Again I wondered if I was finally out matched.

Now I could hear rapids. We were nearing a tributary or the river itself and who could tell without a map and compass. Trouble halted at the river showing no sign of turning either north or south. I had a feeling that Mike had reached the rapids during the day and crossed here. The rapids were very loud here. That meant shallow water. I decided to risk a call to base while the noise of the water hid my voice. I explained the situation as briefly as possible. I also informed them that I planned on walking all night if necessary to narrow the gap. Harold got on the horn and said to be careful and that his prayers would be with me.

I took the lead and crossed the ankle deep water along a line of slippery stones. The stones were sticking out of the water here. The moss was off one of them like Mike had been walking on them and slipped off the bare one. With any luck, he had fallen in. Then he could be as miserable as I was. He, too, was in short sleeves. The dog followed me confidently to the far shore where he once again picked up the trail like I expected. Trouble took the lead again traveling a little more slowly. That was fine with me. If Mike was getting desperate, he may opt for a shoot out at dawn. He probably expected that I would pursue him all night. He had looked genuinely surprised to find out that I was a cop.

If I caught up to him tonight he would be as dead as in the morning. With that thought I continued to follow Trouble through the foggy blackness and hoped that I could surprise my ruthless foe.

I'll have to give him credit for going this far without getting caught. Evidently Crete didn't have any infrared equipment on their helicopter since it wasn't in the air. My friend who was supposed to walk the east bank was probably in bed now. That just meant that he had no chance to capture who must surely be America's most wanted fugitive.

The hours passed slowly, but pass they did and Trouble never alerted again. My arms were inside the T-shirt again. My feet were wet, I was as hungry as the dog and I had the kind of exhaustion that only comes with high stress levels maintained for a long time.

The trail started to go uphill now. The brush thinned out, but the trees closed in thickly. Still, the dog kept on like he had a clear scent. The fog showed little sign of clearing and the temperature was dropping like it always does around dawn. There were worse things than being cold. Watching that snuff movie was the kind of thing that made being cold seem like a romp in the park.

he screams of that crooked cop as he was lowered in the pool full of alligators were still ringing in my ears. That trip down memory lane renewed my energy.

Up ahead, I heard something crashing through the brush off the trail. Either Mike had scared something or vice versa. Trouble slowed down and kept his nose to the ground. A little farther ahead, the dog turned off the trail and headed north through the dense pine forest. So it was Mike who had given up the right of way, probably to a bear. Here the pine needles were thick. I could follow Mike's progress by ear, as he snapped the dry lower branches and cleared a trail for us. The needles muffled the sound of footfalls, while the snapping branches made my job almost as easy as if the sun had come out.

The dog and I were gaining on our quarry. We were within pistol shot but it was still too dark. There was a glow in the eastern sky promising that shot very soon.

Then the branches quit snapping and I could literally hear his ragged breathing as he took a break. I halted the dog, making him lay down, and crawled toward the sounds of panic. I sensed him before I could see him. He was sitting down, leaning against a tree with a pistol in each hand. I lay down and spoke out of the darkness. I told him to drop it. He chose death by cop rather than death by electric chair, firing both pistols at once. He wound up getting shot with the pistol he'd given me as well as my revolver.

Trouble came up to sniff Mike's body. He came back and lay by me as I called base with a "mission accomplished." I told them that the tributary with the rapids would have to be the recovery point since the trees were too close together everywhere else. I told them to send the chopper at dawn and I would have the body there waiting.

I picked Mike up in a fireman's carry, putting up with the pain and risking my stitches, then retraced our route to the trail. Trouble ran off the small bear that cost Mike his life. The evil man's soul was gone a long time ago.

The helicopter was fast approaching in the dawn light. The timing should be perfect. I dumped the body at the shore and waded out in the stream waving my arms. They lowered a litter basket for Mike and another for the dog, who had to be strapped down. They lowered a "Penetrater" for me. I unfolded the arms and had a seat clinging to the cable with a gun in each of my four pockets. The chopper ride was a lot faster than the hellish walk. Even in the cooler weather, the mosquitoes were bad. We were going in a straight line now to downtown Granger. The helicopter set us down in the square. Harold and Jim were awake and anxious to see an end to this nightmare. Like I wasn't?

There were no mourners for Mike as he was carted off to the morgue. Anyone who might have cared was either locked up or dead. I told them that after I took the dog home and fed him, I would meet them at the diner. Peggy was at the door saying that the helicopter woke her. I gave her a quick briefing as I fed Trouble and told her about the meeting at the diner. Then I kissed her goodbye and went to the restaurant to see my friends.

The diner was crowded as only a restaurant with no competition can be. Many of these people drove to Crete to get to their jobs. Happily, most were here for coffee and a roll to go. I spotted my friends in a corner table and waded through the crowd to join them. As I sat down, they both started to talk at once. It sounded like a bidding war for my talents. "Gentlemen, don't I even get a cup of coffee for spending the night in a T-shirt with only a dog, a bear and a murderer for company? I still don't have my stitches out."

Harold said that the Fed was picking up the tab for the whole of the medical costs.

Jim said that I was covered under the county plan. "Remember that you were sworn in a long time ago."

Harold was quick to say, "You have been on our more generous payroll since we discovered that we were dealing in multiple murders."

I said that I didn't want to go to school far away for either job. The Sheriff offered to wave the schooling in Crete.

The FBI man said that I could fly to Virginia and back, and it was only a couple of months training.

I shook Harold's hand goodbye. I told Jim we had a deal. It was done. Now, to make my report. Both men had tape recorders out. I detailed all of the elements of the pursuit up to the extraction of the body. Then they fought over who was buying breakfast while I was eating.

. . .

I contacted my landlord in town and asked if he would sell. He threw a reasonable price at me right off, like he had it in his mind to sell all along. I had about sixteen grand in equity in my double wide and the land. I could make it with a new mortgage on the trailer and rent it out to cover those payments. The house in Granger would suit all of my purposes better.

Jim sold me the dog, Trouble, for one dollar. I had to promise to use him on all local operations. My new love, Peggy, continued to live with her parents until the wedding. Our first born were twin boys. We named them James and Harold.

# ABOUT THE AUTHOR

Erick was born in Chicago in 1948. His last home in The Windy City was a housing project at Sacremento and Harrison. He went to high school in Fox Lake, Illinois before completing one semester as a Biology major at Whitewater, Wisconsin. Prior to serving in the Army, Erick completed a course titled "Modern Construction Techniques" at IIT in Crystal Lake, Illinois. Night school in Grayslake, Illinois added to his knowledge of Carpentry and general construction after his honorable discharge. He furthered his education as an Infantryman for two years in the US Army. As a Pointman in Vietnam with the 101st Airborne, he earned a Combat Infantry Badge, a Bronze Star, an Air Medal, an Army Commendation Medal, and other awards. He spent his adult life alternating between Carpentry and Roofing having worked as a foreman and superintendant respectively. The writer in him was never formally educated nor encouraged. Rather, it was something he'd always wanted to do as he felt that he had a natural talent. Married and living in Dover, Tennessee with his wife Mikki, he has five dogs, ten chickens, a rooster, three snakes and many friends. The father of two natural children and four step-children, he claims kinship to 15 grandchildren and hopes to live long enough to be a great grandfather. Baptized Catholic as a child, he drifted away from The Lord for too many years. Erick is now a born again Christian and was re-baptized at Bear Spring Baptist Church in Dover, Tennessee. Erick states, "I consider my most important responsibility to be raising my children as Christians."